FLOWERS FROM THE MASTER'S GARDEN

THE DREA SERIES
BOOK ONE
By
Andrea Jenkins

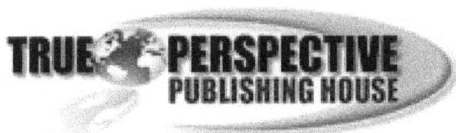

TRUE PERSPECTIVE PUBLISHING HOUSE

Flowers from the Master's Garden
Printed in the United States of America

ISBN 978-0-9975539-7-0

Autograph Page

Grow where you are planted....

ABOUT THE AUTHOR

"No matter what season of life you're in, God allows seeds to be planted so that flowers will grow, adding His Divine beauty to your life."

Andrea Jenkins is a God-inspired writer who has gained wisdom and insight through experiences and lessons that God has used to direct her path, and which she shares with others. Andrea's goal is simple: to share her transparent stories so that others will be encouraged! Some lessons in life come with tears, heartbreak and sorrow, but in the same way that dead leaves on a tree make way for a fuller, healthier tree, so do our trials, dead leaves and limbs fall off to make room for more of God, a stronger, healthier walk and relationship with Him.

Andrea resides in Chesapeake, Virginia where she serves as Director of Family Ministries at the Community United Methodist Church in Virginia Beach. Andrea is a soloist, Praise and Worship leader as well as a songwriter. In addition to various awards in writing and music, Andrea is also an Events Decorator and custom designs accessories for various events. Andrea earned degrees in Social Work and Early Education and is currently working towards her certification as a CPR/First Aid Instructor.

With all Andrea's accomplishments over the years, her greatest and most precious treasure is her son Rahjon, who is the pride and joy of her life!

A NOTE OF THANKS

To God be the glory! I am so honored that God has given the gift of writing to me so I can share the awesomeness of God with those whom He has called me to serve!! I don't take the charge lightly, and I understand that the words He gives me to say impacts lives. My desire is that every word within these pages will bless, encourage and remind you that through every circumstance God is there through it all!

To my family: My son Rahjon Amir DarRell Stallworth, who I love, adore and cherish!! Thank You for always believing in Mommy and letting me know how much you love me! I am so very blessed to be your mother and thank God for gifting me with such a precious son!

To my parents the late Elder Ronald and Evang. Mildred Jenkins, I appreciate you both and all you instilled in me!! Thank you for your words of encouragement, the years of prayers and the words spoken in and over my life!! I am blessed to be your daughter.

Thank You to my sister Tara, my brother- in-law Terrell, nephews Andrew and Daniel; and niece, Bethany-Grace, thank you for your love and encouragement, which is a constant reminder that I can make it through Christ who gives me strength!

God has placed some special people in my life that I love more than I will ever be able to express. To Melea Caldwell "Lefty", my spiritual twin, a woman who has listened to me, allowed me to cry, allowed me to be transparent, and who always has a solid word of wisdom for me. To Tony Robinson, who always seems to hear the words that come through my spirit. To Jennifer Soranio, who always has a word of love and encouragement for me. And Angela Pernell, who has been blessed with the gift of faith and who always speaks faith to me and encourages me to activate my faith all the more!! These women are such a blessing to me! I have such a heart for them, and I thank God for placing them in my life.

To George Jones III, who stepped in to help me parent my son, who has been a blessing not only to him but to me as well!! I appreciate you more than you'll ever know!!

To my Pastor Dr. Melvin O. Marriner and Lady Shelley; thank you for always encouraging me to strive for more in God! Thank you for allowing me to serve in ministry and for encouraging me to be everything that God has called me to be!! I love you both, more than you know. I am encouraged by you! over the last few years, words will never begin to describe the impact you have had on my life. You may not know the details of how your lives are a testimony to me but believe me when I say my heart is so very thankful!!

To every person who has impacted my life: from my supporters to my haters, to my co-workers, to those that hurt me, those that loved me; and to those whom I serve beside in ministry, without the various roles you played in my life I would not be here to stand and share with authority that which God has ordained me to share!!

TABLE OF CONTENTS

Chapter 1

Saving Me FROM Me

I was talking to a friend this morning, and as we were talking a thought came to mind. Think about all the things that invaded your mind over the years; things you wanted to do "just because." Things you wanted to do out of hurt, things that came to mind when you (real talk) were pissed off, those old addictions you could have fallen back into due to your emotions. God is awesome in that He saves us from attacks of the Devil and people, but have you considered that many times God saves us from ourselves?! Think of all the things that we would like to do that God redirects us from so we won't fall into something we didn't bargain for!!

I am not a woman who gets angry often, I may get hurt, and I may get upset, but true anger is not an emotion I experience often. When I do, best believe it is something huge and not the norm. Several years ago, I experienced a situation that had me ENRAGED AND hurt at the same time!! Hurt I could relate to but being completely enraged was something I wasn't familiar with and I was volatile!! I recall lying on my couch trying to settle down, but not being able to because pictures were flashing across my mind of how I could attack the source of my rage!! I was experiencing emotions that I had never encountered before, haven't since, and pray I NEVER will again!! I recall falling asleep and waking up several hours later still hurt, but not enraged. I remember having an "it is what it is" attitude.

As I think back to that day, I know without a doubt that had it not been for God's soothing balm, I would be in prison today!! One small moment in my life would have destroyed it if God had not saved Andrea from Andrea!! I would have been in prison; not jail, but PRISON living my life confined or perhaps on death row. My parents would have been heartbroken, and my son, I shudder to think what his life would have been like!

God's grace protects us from things that are out of our control, but God also spends a lot of time shielding us FROM us! Even when we make choices that He has clearly warned us about, He still will shield us from the full impact of our choices, and then He will have His healing balm waiting to soothe us. Growing up I would hear the old folks talk about the balm of Gilead; God's healing balm; but it wasn't until just now, as I thought about that experience that I understood!! God took His healing, soothing balm and applied it to a volatile situation!! He applied it to my mind, my heart, and my spirit!God saved me FROM me!!

There was a song that Andrae Crouch wrote that asked a few questions: "Where would I be if Jesus didn't love me? Where would I be if He did care? Where would I be if He hadn't sacrificed His life?" (I Don't Know Why Jesus Loves Me by Andrae Crouch, The Disciples Album: Keep On Singin')

I'm so thankful for this revelation God gave me today; for allowing me to see how God's awesome love for me has protected me from MY thoughts; thoughts that had not been soothed and extinguished by God's balm would have cost me my life!!

If you really look back at some of the things you thought about doing, let alone the things you did, you wouldn't hesitate but to walk around daily with an attitude of thanksgiving because in asking yourselves those questions you would KNOW where you would be!! You would know if you had done "that" what would have happened. If you had dated her, married him, got back at him or her, you KNOW your life would be completely different! You'd be in jail, prison, living on death row, in the psych ward, abused, an alcoholic, or lying in the cemetery!! You KNOW!! BUT God!! He didn't allow your thoughts, MY thoughts, to become reality!! Without the healing balm of God, I KNOW I would be in prison, I KNOW I could be in a mental hospital due to other situations I experienced, etc.

God shielded my mind from the thoughts that could have led to devastating actions! SINGING, "I don't know why Jesus loved me, I don't know why He cares, I don't know why He sacrificed His life, Oh but I'm glad, so glad He did!" We truly don't know the vastness of God's love for us; our minds are not equipped to understand and comprehend!! God's love cannot be compared to any other love we experience!!

God sees beyond our limited ability. He sees what our choices could potentially do to us, and how we can destroy our own lives, but His love reaches out to cover us!! There is another song that says, "There IS no greater love...No greater love..." ("No Greater Love", by the Georgia Mass Choir, 25th Anniversary Gospel Music Workshop)

I'm so thankful for this revelation God gave me today; for allowing me to see how God's awesome love for me has protected me from MY thoughts; thoughts that had not been soothed and extinguished by God's balm would have cost me my life!!

Chapter 2

The Lesson In A Hem

As I thought about the awesomeness of God this week, my mind kept going back to the story of the woman with the issue of blood.The Word she touched the "hem" (Mathew 9:21) of His garment, not the sleeve, not the collar; The HEM. When we think about a hem, we think about the area at the bottom of a garment that has been completed, and it is sewn so not to unravel! So, the woman had to be close to the ground to touch the hem!

When we are at the bottom of the barrel, when we are at our lowest point, we only have to grab what is within our reach! Even the hem, what we may see as being at the bottom of Jesus, has power!! I don't have to be in the face of Jesus to receive a miracle, I can be crawling on the ground and receive my deliverance just by clutching the hem!! (Oh my God!!)

The second thing God placed on my spirit was this: the hem of an outfit is sewn usually when the garment is finished. This woman had been to many doctors and used up all her money, but nothing that was done ended her suffering. Nothing sealed or dried up her issue, her issue continued. Her suffering didn't come to an end until she touched the hem. The hem represented the end of her suffering. Her suffering was over! When we reach out to touch the hem of Jesus' garment, we can expect all that we have experienced to end! It's done, finished! When God puts a period at the end of something, it is sealed never to return!!

Thirdly, the hem of a garment is designed not to unravel; it is designed to keep the rest of the outfit intact. The hem keeps threads from hanging and undoing all the work that had been put into creating the outfit in the first place. When God seals something, puts an end to something, or completes something, we do not have to fear the old issues coming back! He doesn't leave loose threads that may unravel all the healing that had taken place. Satan may try to make things look as if old issues have returned and may send symptoms to trick us into doubting God's ability to do a complete job in our lives. But God does not half do anything, and anything He seals and completes is never to return. We may experience NEW issues, but that which God ended is ended! The woman with the blood issue was completely healed; she never returned to the state from which she had been healed. It was over! And likewise, when God says issues are over in our lives, we can rest and be at peace that it is over, never to return, never to haunt us!!

I am thankful for this lesson and revelation. As God is allowing me to turn the corner, I can trust in the fact that I don't have to return to the areas from where God has taken me. I don't have to return to the doors that God has closed. Satan may try to show me little strings, but the same way we cut off the strings that hang on an outfit instead of pulling them, I can cut off those little strings that Satan may use to try to get me to pull. The pulling will cause the things that God had sealed to unravel!! Sub-Lesson: Don't unravel the things in our lives that God has sealed and ended!!

Sometimes we are barely holding on, things are piled up, the piles have piles... BUT if we can just take hold to the hem of God's garment, He will show Himself! The woman with the issue of blood didn't grab on to a sleeve; she was at the bottom. She was on the ground and took hold of what she could. His hem!! A little bit of Jesus; a little bit of faith is all we need to get the deliverance we need!! Grab hold to the hem, and don't let go. See if God doesn't prove Himself to you!!

I appreciate God taking the time to minister to me on the backend of this season in my life! My desire is not to return to the former things. Lord, help me to apply the lesson and allow it to take root in me!

Chapter 3

A Lesson/A Word of Correction on What It Means To "WAIT" On God

I was lying in my bed, unable to sleep or rest because my mind and spirit were in a battle. I had gone to church earlier and I heard a word that I should have been able to apply, but yet I was in a state of unrest and could not come out of it. As I lay there, I decided to inbox a friend of mine who I knew would say something that would help quiet my spirit. As I began to pour out what was going on with me, I made the statement that I was having a hard time rising and flying above the storm. It was at that point that God began to minister to my spirit.

Some of us are familiar with Isaiah 40:31: "But they that wait upon the LORD shall renew their strength, they shall mount up with wings as eagles; they shall run and not be weary; and they shall walk, and not faint." As I lay across my bed with tears streaming down my face, God spoke this verse into my spirit. My first response was to ask, *'What do I do while I'm waiting? Do I just "stand" there?'* God then reminded me that "waiting" does not mean to be inactive, but to serve Him, and cater to Him. God gave me the analogy of a restaurant where the wait staff is there to serve and cater to the customers. God showed me that customers do not go to the wait staff, but the wait staff goes to the customers. God let me know that in waiting on Him, I need to go to Him, and not the other way around. That made sense, but in my frustrated state I said to God, *'But God, I am coming to you, and I am going to where you are' and that is where the correction came* (SMH). God said, as clear as day, *'Yes Andrea, You come to me, but You don't come to serve or wait on me; you come to complain and cry!!!'* WHEW!!!

God let me know that when I wait on Him, when I serve Him, or render unto Him my gifts, that is when He will give me strength. God showed me how He resides above the storm, so when as a servant I go to where He is with the purpose of serving, waiting, and catering to Him, I will be operating above my situation, above my circumstance!! The storm may still be taking place, but because I have gone to where He is with the purpose of serving, I can be like the eagle rising above the storm, not walking in frustration, fear, and doubt!!

God let me know that although I come to Him, my position was wrong, and that when you serve it has to be a positive action. Good wait staff do all they can to accommodate the customer; they don't complain about the other waiters, nor do they tell you that the food is bad. Their goal is to make your dining experience as positive as possible, and as a reward for good service they receive a tip. God showed me that although I give Him praise and bless Him in church, and I talk and share Him with others, when it comes to that one-on-one time, I did not give Him good service, and that I had not been worthy of a "tip." While God sees my heart and knows my intent, sometimes intent isn't good enough, there has to be effort and execution!!! It is not good enough for me to rely on God knowing what I'm going through. I have to provide good service no matter what!! It doesn't matter that I got up on the wrong side of the bed, my son deserves my best as his mother; my students deserve me at my best as their teacher.

When I approach God, if I am serving Him, waiting on Him, and catering to Him, then He deserves my best service, and my best service does not include complaining, crying, and telling God what He already knows over and over. God let me know that what He has for me is already in place; my "tip" has been calculated, but in the same way as a teacher I do not give my students treats when their behavior is not on track, I cannot expect God to bless me with what He already promised me if I continue to moan, cry, and complain over something He ALREADY said was mine, simply because I don't have it yet. God let me know that the reason I don't have what He promised yet is BECAUSE I am crying and complaining over not having it!! In other words, my spirit has been like that of the prodigal son, who complained over something that already belonged to him!! Needless to say, this was a hard one to hear, but who God loves He corrects, so while all ten of my toes are sore, and because I was" knocked to the ground" my fingers got crunched as well, I understand and appreciate God's hand of correction!!!!!
My true desire is to be a woman of integrity, a woman of whom God can be proud, and that I know there has to be a cutting away, changing, and the adding of stuff!!

Lord, as much as You know I love You, I repent for not being the waitress I should have been, after all You have done in my life over the years, and how You kept my mind through some serious issues over the years is worth me always coming to You with a spirit of thanksgiving!!! Forgive me Lord!!! I thank You so much for the opportunity to clean up and step up so that I can be the woman of service, the waitress, and the woman of integrity You've called me to be, the woman in You I desire to be.

I pray that as you read my early morning experience, you will evaluate your wait service to God so that you can avoid my error. I thought about the times when I've gone to restaurants and was asked to evaluate the service, and to evaluate the wait staff by using a rating system. I just experienced God rating me, and my service to God was unacceptable. I thought I was serving God well; I thought I was just being honest with God at where I was, but in reality, I had a spirit of complaining. I was coming to God on my private time not to serve but to beef about something He already said was mine!! Because of His mercy and because of His grace I have the opportunity to serve Him again and strive for better. The good news is that in sharing my experience, God has given an opportunity for all of us to conduct self-evaluations, and if need be, make the corrections in our lives!!!

Chapter 4

Being Where God Says To Be

You can't get what God wants you to have if you're not where God told you to be! If blessings and favor are "here" don't expect God to send them "over there" if He told your hind parts to stay "here!" How many times have we had to tell our children to stay "here" or go sit "over there" just to turn around for a quick second and when we look back they are gone!! God is no different in this respect as we are with our children, if God said, 'Sit there and wait' then that is what He means! My mom used to say to Tara and me as children, "I mean what I say." God means what He says!!

How can we say to God, "Order my steps in Your Word, Dear Lord; lead me, guide me everyday day..." and then when He begins to order our steps we deliberately go in another direction? How much sense does that make? We may as well have not wasted our breath! But yet we plead with God, "Pleassssssssssssssse order my steps in Your word, Pleasssssssssssssssssse order my steps in Your Word." I'm sure the Lord at times is like, "Yeah whatever! You're not gonna listen to me anyway." -smh-

Sampson was messed up for going "over there." His blessing wasn't "over there" but the agent who was used for his downfall was "over there." David was "out there" in the field tending his sheep where he was supposed to be, so when the prophet came looking for the next king his father knew just where David would be: "out there" tending sheep. Ruth knew her place was to "stay there" with Naomi, not to go "back there" like Orpah. Ruth's blessing wasn't "back there" but "up there" with Naomi.

We have to know our place and know where God has called us to be. For years I wanted to leave Virginia and return to Atlanta. Every year I would tell my co-workers that this would be my last year at school, and I was going back to Georgia. HOWEVER, I have come to realize that what God had for my life wasn't located in Georgia; it's located in Virginia. The blessing may relocate to Georgia at some point, but for this season my place is here in Virginia. When God is finished with me here, then I will go to the next location that He has for me.

If you're already "where" God has called you to be, STAND STILL AND SEE THE SALVATION OF THE LORD. BUT, if you're not "where" God has called you to be, my advice is that you hurry up and get "there!" TO HAVE WHAT GOD HAS, YA GOTTA BE WHERE HE SAYS YOU NEED TO BE!!

Chapter 5

A Lesson In Little Pebbles

Have you ever been out walking somewhere and you trip or stumble a bit? You did not stumble enough to make you fall, but just enough for you to fear losing your balance. Yet, when you looked down to see what you tripped over, you don't see anything. Whatever you tripped over was so small that you couldn't detect the culprit. Often in our Christian walk it's not the huge things that cause us to lose balance, but the small things that seem to have little significance, or the tiny stuff that catches us off-guard so quickly that we almost don't realize that something has taken place.

One of the greatest shortcomings of those of us who walk with Christ is underestimating the tactics of the devil. We don't always remember that he is very strategic and deliberate in his actions and takes time to study us before launching an attack. Satan knows what will get us going; he knows that we won't outright steal, but he knows that if a salesclerk gives us too much change back we may not say anything. We may not say openly how much we think someone has received something we want or we think that we deserved it more than they did, but when we see someone getting the attention we believe that we deserved and desired, the little green-eyed monster will arise from the deep!! It's not the big boulders in our way that will cause us to lose focus, but it's those small, subtle things that can cause us to take our eyes off God just enough to where regaining focus may take some effort.

A few days ago, I experienced that little "pebble in the road." My natural eye saw something that disturbed me and caused me to focus on it and brought on insecurities that I work on daily. What I saw was so slight, what I saw was by "accident," but it had enough of an impact to cause me to trip, but not enough to fall. I had to refocus my attention, center myself, collect my emotions and redirect my focus from what my natural eyes saw to what God had shown me.

Now a few days later I see how something so small, just a glimpse, just a moment of doubt, just a flash of a lie could turn our entire focus upside down if we're not careful. Satan doesn't put those huge distractions in our view to take our eyes off God, or to cause doubt; all he has to do is throw a little hint of something, a little doubt, or a little nudge on our self-esteem. He doesn't have to hit us with a huge bat; he can just poke us with a stick just at the right time to cause a domino effect in our lives, and the closer we get to our "Promised Land," the more that Satan will try these little cheap shots that can cause delays in our manifestation. We don't have to lose faith in God completely to get off track. A small dose of doubt, a small hint of fear, a teaspoon of jealousy or anger, or a slight outburst, can cause great damage. Have you ever noticed a small crack in your windshield, a slight dent in your bumper, or a nick to your paint job?? It wasn't a huge rock that caused this; often times it was a tiny pebble that hit your car just at the right angle at just the right time, and at just the right speed, but a pebble that has now caused damage that will now take a lot of money to repair.

Perhaps you've had the experience of spraining an ankle. You were walking along and something tiny hit your foot at a certain angle, which caused you to slip and twist your foot. You didn't fall, and you didn't break your ankle, but that slip, that moment of being caught unaware now has your foot in an ace bandage, propped up with ice. Those little things can cause big headaches, and a great deal of unnecessary pain and frustration.

Many of us are so close to the promise, to "that thing" that God spoke into our spirits that we cannot allow the "tiny stuff" to tip us over. More than ever, we have to keep our minds and hearts protected. We have to condition ourselves to use our spiritual senses and not allow our eye, ear, and mouth gates to be infiltrated by those tiny virus germs that can have us lying on our spiritual sick beds, wondering what happened.

This was a lesson I experienced and I wanted to share it with you to encourage you to remain alert, to activate your spiritual motion detectors, to be aware that it's not always the big attacks on our lives that will bring us to a place of instability, and that we need to be mindful and watchful of the more sneaky and low-key ways that Satan may try to worm his way into our camp. None of us can afford to allow the slightest distraction to overtake us. We have to stay on constant alert, always on guard, and quick on our feet to recognize those little things that may be the thing that will cause our eyes to lose focus.

I encourage you today to look at things through your spiritual bifocals, and listen with your spiritual hearing aids, and speak using the proper spiritual dialect. The devil may have weapons formed, but they don't have to take us over; they don't have to prosper. The key is to be spiritually aware and spiritually alert.

Chapter 6

A Strong Poker Face

I'm not a card player, as no good "Jesus Only" raised "In the Way" Pentecostal would ever engage in such games of chance, especially if money is a factor (smile): but in any good card game, from Uno to Poker, the key to winning is having the ability to outsmart those also at the table. Specifically in the game of Poker, one must have the ability to do two things: one, have the ability to keep ones' hand a secret from the other players in the game,   and two, maintain a strong Poker face.

In the "Poker Game" of life, if you intend to beat the devil's attempt to sabotage your game, it is crucial and critical that you keep your hand hidden from him, and to always maintain a strong Poker face. In other words, don't give the devil ammunition to use against you by allowing him to see your strengths and your weaknesses. He will turn around and attempt to destroy you with them. It's one thing for the devil to come against us with the agenda to kill, steal, and destroy, but it's a completely different story when we sabotage ourselves by literally handing him the tools, utensils, floor plans, maps, combinations to the safe, and the master key with which to do so. The devil doesn't care who or what he uses to destroy us; whatever vessel is available is what he will use. If someone robs your home, that's one thing, but why invite a thief to rob your house by leaving the key in the lock?

I'm not there yet, but I'm learning that sometimes rather than venting my hurts, frustrations, insecurities and shortcomings, sometimes it's best to just keep silent, or if I must share them, share them with God who will always protect that which we lay at His feet. On the flip side, if I do opt to share, I'm learning to be very selective with whom I share. Oftentimes the devil will use those who are close to us to bring about our destruction.

Not to say men don't do this, but this behavior is more commonly found in women (sad, but true). Have you ever witnessed a woman sharing certain "private" information and details about their spouse or significant other with their female friends, the details that should be kept exclusive? "TMI" information shared with a girlfriend who more often then not will be the same girlfriend who will later betray or replace the woman originally thought sharing with her gurl was a good idea, and who thought that bragging about her man would make her gurl envy her, was not thinking that what she bragged about is the very thing her gurl used to get her man. Perhaps you've come across some information, whether it be in business, about a house that hasn't hit the market yet, or some other opportunity, and you casually mention to it to a family member just to have them slip in and steal it from right under you. Again, I have not reached perfection in this area, but more and more I am learning not to share everything, good or bad, and to be very selective with whom I do share.

As I look at the circumference of people I share with, I've noticed over the last year that the radius has become much smaller. In certain situations, God literally showed me that I couldn't trust certain friends with everything, because even good information can be used against you since everyone in your circle won't "rejoice with them that rejoice." Even with those whom I KNOW I can trust with information, I'm slowly but surely learning to sift through what I share. There are certain times in my life when my frustrations, lack of patience, insecurities and need to vent overwhelm me and I find myself like a broken dam bursting with water. In those times, more and more, I'm hearing the gentle voice of God reminding me to lay my burdens at His feet and to release to Him, who is and will always be my source of strength. I'm learning the hard lesson that sometimes in silence there is the awesome protection and covering of God.

God has blessed me with a beautiful friend who no matter how much I get on a "pity party" tip she always has a word of love and encouragement for me. Even in the gift of her friendship, and even with the knowledge that she covers me in love and in prayer, she is my friend; a friend with limited human abilities. If I want to see my prayers become reality, my questions answered, my heart uplifted, or miracles manifested, God is the only one who can produce results.

I'm reminded of the story of Hannah, the mother of Samuel who desired a child. Daily she would go to the temple to pray and petition the Lord to bless her with a child. Here is the beauty of the story; at no time do we read about Hannah going around crying to her girlfriends about being childless. What we do see, however, is Hannah engaging in a private dialog with her God, and because of that one-on- one communication, she was granted her request. What had been a burden; a source of sadness, disappointment, frustration, dishonor as a woman, and what could be considered a curse or thorn in her life was not used against her.

Had she articulated her feelings and added to her emotions, then doubt, discouragement, bad advice, or failure could have been planted in her spirit which would have worked against what she believed God to do for her. Her quiet dialog with God shielded and protected her because the feelings she had were under the covering of God. If you were on the sidelines looking at Hannah, the only thing one could say was that her lips were moving; even in prayer her petitions could not be heard.

In that same vein, Sampson neglected to keep the secret of his strength, and ended up with his head in the lap of the one whom the devil had drafted to bring about his fall. Sampson's anointing was used entrap him. Again, it is one thing to have something taken from you, but it's something totally different to turn something over to the enemy on a silver platter.

As we look at Hannah and Sampson, what difference can we observe between the two? Hannah was a good poker player; she knew what her hand looked like and protected it from onlookers. Hannah understood what was at risk, and she wasn't about to show she possessed a "full house" by revealing her cards, or by the allowing what she was holding to appear on her countenance. Sampson, however, was overly confident that he had the winning hand and taunted those playing with him at the table. He failed to realize that while he may have had a good hand, but Delilah had a better one and thus all he had wagered was now laying in Delilah's lap!! Much like in the story of the Tortoise and the Hare, Sampson lost the game overall by not having a good Poker face. Someone who should have never had the opportunity to obtain the victory won the game.

All of us, at one time or another has heard the expression, "Less Is More." No words could be truer. Satan doesn't care what tools he uses to cause us harm, it doesn't matter if it's a tool he just happens to come across, or if it's a tool we unknowingly give him, it could be a tool that is negative such as our frustrations, weaknesses, or mistakes, or a tool that is positive such as our gifts, talents and anointing. He doesn't care who is available to bring about our downfall from, everyone from family to foe to Satan is fair game so it is up to us not to give him resources to use against us unnecessarily. Since we already know that Satan doesn't play fair, with that knowledge, it becomes our responsibility to protect ourselves, to execute practices that will shield us.

There are things God will do for us, but there are also things we can do for ourselves, so before you willingly hand over the keys to your spiritual limited addition vehicle with the custom paint job and one of a kind rims to Satan knowing that he's going to do all he can to total it, wisdom dictates that you watch what you say, and watch who you say it to. We may not like it, but the reality is that Satan is in this game right along with us, and if you're going to play the game, we must play to win!! So hide your spiritual "hand" and put on your best spiritual "Poker face" if the devil wants to dethrone you, let him work to do so, don't just hand your life over. Don't throw your cards, play your hand, but play it well!!

Chapter 7

It's The Great Pumpkin, Charlie Brown

I always find it interesting and awesome when God takes everyday things and turns them into life lessons. Earlier today I had an opportunity to learn one of these great lessons, and the manner in which God spoke into my spirit is nothing short of awesome!!

You may have spent long periods of time with young children, or perhaps you remember the various holiday Charlie Brown specials. In such a wonderful way, God deposited an awesome word using a wonderful Charlie Brown classic, *"It's The Great Pumpkin Charlie Brown."*

In this story, Charlie Brown's friend Linus is waiting for the coming of The Great Pumpkin, an entity he believes will appear in the pumpkin patch on Halloween night and distribute candy and toys to those who believe. In all of the Charlie Brown specials, Linus is the head of reason; he is the one who keeps Charlie Brown from going completely crazy. For example, in the Christmas special, it's Linus who answers Charlie Brown's question on what the true meaning of Christmas was. Linus took center-stage to share with Charlie Brown that Christmas was about a baby born of a virgin who would be the hope of the world. Linus stood as a testament to wisdom, and common sense, and who was always available to help Charlie Brown through his many periods of confusion, paranoia, and depression. We get to the Halloween special where Linus steps completely out of character to believe in the mystical Great Pumpkin. In all his wisdom, and even with the true knowledge of the birth of Jesus, Linus walks away from all reason to believe that a huge pumpkin was going to rise from the pumpkin patch.

Now here is where the story gets awesome. Despite the fact that only Linus had heard of this Great Pumpkin, despite the fact that he had to sit outside in the cold and wait for him, despite the fact that only one person, Sally believed with him but later turned her back on him, despite the fact that because he chose to wait for the pumpkin to arrive he missed out on trick or treating with his friends, and the Halloween party, Linus was persuaded that the Great Pumpkin WOULD come and would wait until he arrived!! WHEW!!! It didn't matter what it looked like; Linus decided that no matter who believed with him, who laughed at him, or who doubted, HE was going to sit in the pumpkin patch until the Great Pumpkin came. Linus forsook "reason" to believe what others looked at as foolishness!! The normal, clear-minded Linus chose to look crazy in front of his friends for the sake of a huge orange pumpkin...and even further, Linus didn't care how he looked; he believed, and that was that - end of discussion.

WOW!!! How many of us have heard from God on various things in our lives, but when we don't see the manifestation, we abandon what we KNOW God said. How many of us waver when those close to us don't see or understand what we're believing God for? How many of us become hurt and offended because people around us laugh or speak against what we're believing God to do for us? If God said it...

that settles it! We have to stand on the Word of a God who not only doesn't lie, but also who is unable to lie!!

Now look at this.... (This revelation here was awesome to me) at the end of the story, the Great Pumpkin never appeared. It seemed that Linus had waited for nothing, and that what he believed was a lie. To the naked, untrained, and unspiritual eye, Linus had fallen for a big lie. But look at the stance that Linus took. His last word on the matter was, next year he was going to be out there waiting again for the Great Pumpkin to come!! So what, he didn't appear this year, but there is always next year, and the year after that, and the year after that!!! Linus had made up his mind that no matter how long it takes, he was going to wait until the Great Pumpkin came!!!

This was a word for me!! No matter what it looks like, I must stand still and wait for God to manifest what He promised for my life. I will not allow conditions and circumstances to shake me from what I know God had said to me. I will. not to allow the words of doubting friends to sway me.

If God has spoken a word into your spirit, no matter what it is, how big it is, how hard it is, how unqualified you think you are, how unattainable it may appear to be, how out of your league people may say you are.... STAND!! Don't allow yourself to miss what God has for you because of self- doubt or the doubt of others. If God said it, and you know He said it, then sit tight and wait in your spiritual pumpkin patch until YOUR "Great Pumpkin" rises to manifest itself in your life!! Take a lesson from Linus: no matter what, don't move, don't waver, don't doubt.... Believe and hold fast until you see something happen on your behalf. Wait for YOUR GREAT PUMPKIN!!

Chapter 8

My Birthday Testimony

I celebrate my birthday on November 27th, and I'm so grateful for God's hand of mercy and grace over my life. I try to share this testimony of God's love and grace every year in some form with the hope and prayer that as my "Birthday Testimony" is read, someone will be encouraged and blessed, and would know that God has a purpose for each of your lives. You are an investment to Him and God will go to the limit to protect the life He has called into His service.

I celebrate every birthday because there was a time in my life when I didn't think I would live to see 21, let alone live to see anything past that, but while I didn't see it at the time, God had a calling on my life that would not allow me to be destroyed by the hand of the enemy.

When I was getting ready to turn 21, that year my birthday fell on Thanksgiving Day and I was involved with a young man who lived some distance from me. Several times a week I would travel back and forth to spend time with him. At the same time, I was also singing and ministering with the group Love Divine, a group that I had been singing with for some time and who I was committed to, and I loved being a part of the group very much. One evening, my friend asked me to come to where he was to spend some time with him. I agreed, but I told him that I wouldn't be able to be there until late because I had a rehearsal. Needless to say, he wasn't happy with my decision, and told me that if I didn't get to where he was by a certain time I would be locked out. I did think that he meant that literally, so I didn't give it a second thought and continued with my plans to go to rehearsal.

Well on this particular evening the Lord swept through our rehearsal! The rehearsal became an evening of praise and worship, and God's hand was on each of us. The room was thick with His anointing, and rehearsal lasted much longer than what was typical for us. After rehearsal was over, I got in my car and drove to where my friend stayed, and what was normally an hour and a half drive was cut down to 45 minutes. I was driving up the highway at 80-100 miles an hour trying to get to my destination before the doors were "locked on me."

Once I got up there I ran up four flights of stairs trying to make my mandate just to get to the door to hear the bolt being put on the door. I knocked, I cried, I begged, but the door remained locked. He had really locked me out and wasn't trying to let me in!! At that moment the plan the devil had for me began to take shape. I was hurt; self-esteem issues that I had dealt with during the relationship and prior began to come back, and a situation that should have been minor, a situation I should not have cared about, a situation I should have just walked away from with the reality that he was not who God had for me took on a whirlwind effect and my emotions of being rejected and left out in the November Boston cold began to blow.

At that the of the night/early morning I had no idea what to do, I didn't have enough money for a hotel, and even at age 20, there was no way I could walk into Elder and Sis Jenkins house that late. I got in my car and just began driving, not having a plan, but knew I had to do something.

As I was driving, I began to cry uncontrollably, I couldn't believe that my "friend" cared so little about me, a man who had talked to me about marriage. I meant nothing to him, I meant so little that he would lock me out late at night and not give my welfare a second thought! I was on the highway alone and so overcome with hurt that I could barely see the road. As I was driving, I came to an area where the road took a sharp curve, on the left there was a guardrail that protected drivers from a steep rocky cliff. It was at that time I heard Satan's voice clearly say, "Andrea, if you drive your car through this guard rail and off the cliff, you wouldn't die; you would only hurt yourself just enough to make him feel guilty and treat you better."

In all my pain, at the time that made sense, I didn't want to die, but I did want him to feel bad for hurting me. (SN: How many of you know that part of the devil's tricks is to make things "look" like, or "seem" like it makes sense when you are in a state of hurt?) So I proceeded to pick up speed with the intention of driving my car off this cliff, I got right to the guard rail and prepared myself for the impact knowing that I was not going to die, (I didn't want that) but knowing that I WAS going to be hurt, suddenly "something" took control of the steering wheel and steered the car across 4 lanes and parked the car on the opposite side of the road in the breakdown lane.

I turned off the car, put my head down on the steering wheel and just began to sob, it was then I heard the voice of the Lord say to me... "But Andrea I love you, and I will never leave you." It was at that moment I realized that God had just saved me from Satan's lie!! That night Satan intended to kill me; his mission was to steal, kill and destroy me! Yes, my friend might have felt guilty, but his guilt would have been over my DEATH, not because I got hurt!! A few days later, on Thanksgiving Day I turned 21, and God let me know that He had preserved my life for a special purpose, and from that birthday until this one, I have always been grateful to God for his awesome grace and mercy.

While I still continue to experience the ups and downs of life, every year I take the moment to celebrate my birthday. For me, it's a day of thanksgiving because I KNOW that if not for God, my family would mourn for me every year on this day, rather than celebrate with me the mighty things God has done and continues to do in my life.

So, on each birthday as I walk into another year of my life, I am so grateful to God for all He has done in, with, and through me!! I mess up, I make mistakes, but I can never deny God's hand and His calling over my life...and for that alone, on my birthday I smell every flower that God allows mc to experience, and I treasure my moments for I know that had it not been for Him I would not be here sharing this testimony!!

Chapter 9

Air Circulation

Sometimes the climate in my classroom is one of complete confusion!! One child is hitting, one child is whining, one child is being bossy, and still another child simply just wants to go home!!! When those days come, and when even I want to go home and have Calgone moment, that's when I stop everything that is going on and call for an EXHALE MOMENT. This moment where my students know exactly what we are about to do, and they are very aware of why we are going to do it. An Exhale moment is when I tell my students that we all need to calm down. "It's time to bring it down," I would tell them. We would all inhale a big gulp of air and release it. I tell my students, "In with the good air, out with the bad air," and after a few times of doing it, emotions have settled down, and the positive climate of my classroom has been restored.

Sometimes there is some much going on in our lives to the point where we get completely overwhelmed with the demands and stress that is a part of our daily living. When those times come, we need to step back and take a SPIRITUAL EXHALE MOMENT. Moments where we release all the tension, all the stress, and all the mess and let God refill our spiritual lungs with refreshing air.

Have you ever been in a room that doesn't have windows, or where the windows don't open? A room that is stuffy and stale? Perhaps you have been someplace where people have been smoking and that smoke is circulating overhead. Now think how your physical body feels when you're in that type of environment. You're groggy, sleepy, lazy. If you are in a work environment, you can't concentrate or focus, the day seems to drag on.

It feels more like an 18-hour workday. Why is that? It's because the air you are breathing in has lost an important component; it has lost a small percentage of oxygen. Oxygen is carried by the blood to the brain and dispersed so that the body can function properly. Without this source of transportation, the body is deprived of what it needs to stay alert. However, once you leave that environment, open a window; go outside, you will notice both your physical and mental condition will change; why? Because the proper dose of oxygen is now flowing through your body.

It is the same in the spiritual realm; if we remain in a stale or stagnant environment, we are depriving our spirits of the elements needed to function. Sometimes we simply have to step back and breathe in the goodness of God and allow Him to breathe back into us those nutrients we are lacking.

Yesterday I was in a spiritual situation that had me gasping for fresh air. The situation had my spiritual lungs so congested that I could hardly breathe. This spiritual state had spilled over into the natural realm, where I was so frustrated and even angry at what was taking place. It was time for a SPIRITUAL EXHALE MOMENT!! It was time for me to remove myself from that stale environment and to breathe in the freshness of God. Now while the situation I was looking at did not change, my condition did. I was able to step back and enjoy the peace and freshness of God and lay aside the stale irritating air that had me choking.

The question one may ask is how do we experience the fresh air of God? How can we get from under the weight of stale air and begin to breathe freely? That is an answer that is unique to everyone. Each of us have a relationship with God that is personal and special, a relationship where we know how to get to Him, and where He knows what has to take place in order to get our attention. For me, fresh air can mean a time of singing, a time when I open up and allow a song to blow over and through me. Other times it's sitting down and writing, exhaling in written form, and inhaling the freshness of understanding while allowing God to minister to me through what He was depositing in me to write. For you it could be a number of things; time spent in prayer, and time reading passages from Psalms. It could be an inspired poem, or it could be a walk where you take time to marvel and acknowledge the awesomeness of God's power. It could even be simply enjoying the peace that quiet brings, where you aren't doing anything at all but just being still. Still, for others it could be a nice bubble bath or that catnap... whatever it is that allows you to exhale the polluted air and allows you the opportunity to enjoy the fresh air of God. All of us need that time of refreshing, it is crucial to the proper functioning of the spiritual body.

I encourage you, if you are feeling weighed down spiritually, if you are feeling spiritually lazy, spiritually sleep deprived, spiritually depressed, spiritually stale, it may be time for a SPIRITUAL

EXHALE MOMENT, a time where you lay aside all the weights and allow the fresh air of God to rejuvenate you and stimulate your spiritual blood flow. BREATHE IN… BREATHE OUT… IN WITH THE GOOD AIR… OUT WITH THE BAD AIR.

Chapter 10

The Gag Gift

The Word declares that God will not withhold any good thing from his children. God is the giver of good gifts; He enjoys seeing His children delight in His blessings. No matter if the gift is a home, a car, that job we prayed for, that spouse, or that child, God smiles when He gives us the things we requested. The same way we enjoy giving our own children gifts, God enjoys the excitement that comes with being the gift giver.

On the other side of that coin, Satan has gifts that he also wants to give us. While God gives us good gifts, Satan's gifts are meant for our harm; they are meant to destroy us. They look good, smell good, taste good, but the end result is nothing but hurt, deception and death.

Have you ever received a gag gift? A gift that was dressed up in pretty paper, complete with a bow? It looked so pretty from the outside, so you thought that there had to be something good inside, right? You opened the gift only to find that someone played a joke on you. While you may laugh, inside you can't help but feel disappointed because you were expecting something different because of how the gift was packaged and displayed. The gift looked good, but the reality was that it wasn't good.

How many times have we received a gift thinking that it was good, but in the end it was meant for our harm? That woman or that man who we thought was a good partner but who turned our lives upside down; that home that we thought was ours but turned out to need more repairs than we thought; that dream job that turned out to cause so much stress, or that car that drained our money in gas, insurance, and upkeep. As children of the King, we have to discern the "gifts" that come our way and recognize WHO is giving the gift. God's gifts do not come with grief, while you can expect Satan's gifts will come with nothing but grief.

Recently I had a conversation with my long-distance Pastor concerning relationships, and he deposited something into me that I've been thinking about a lot. When people come into our lives, we need to ask God what the purpose of them is being there; are they there for our good or are they there to cause grief. That one question will help us to discern if the gift is a good gift, a divine gift, or a gag gift. What is the purpose of this man or woman coming into my life?

Is he/she there as a helpmate, or a burden? Has this job been offered to me as a way to be a blessing to the Kingdom and my family, or has it been offered to me as a way of keeping me out of weekly worship and away from my family? Is this home a way of me being able to show hospitality, or is it a way of bleeding my bank account?

Just because a gift is offered doesn't mean you have to accept it. Accepting a gift is saying that you accept all that comes with it. Not long ago a friend introduced me to her brother. After chatting a bit, he asked if he could get my number and call sometime…Harmless right?? WRONG! The gentleman proceeded to call my house at all hours of the night and early morning and became angry when I would not allow him to spend the night, even though in his words he would sleep on the floor at the end of my bed (smh).

He would fuss me out if he called and I did not answer my phone, even if it was at 5am on a Saturday, or if I didn't pick up my phone while at work. It was very apparent that this was a gag gift, a gift not meant for my good, but meant to bring nothing but stress into my life. (As if I needed more stress!) Well, around the holidays he wanted to buy an expensive gift for me. I told him that I would not accept any gift let alone an expensive one, and why would I when it was clear that the relationship had no possibility of going anywhere. Well, he did not listen to me and opted to purchase the gift anyway. This man became extremely hostile when I not only would not accept the gift, but when I asked him to not contact me any further. It was so unbelievable to me that after only seeing a picture of me (we never met in person) and after only 4 weeks of talking on the phone, he purchased the gift and had his sister deliver it to me!!

Friends, we cannot accept gifts just because they look good to the eye; by doing so we accept the all the disclosures that come with it. While the gift that the gentleman purchased was gorgeous, accepting it would mean that I was accepting him not only to be a part of my life but also to be a part of my son's life. NOT!! There is a saying that says, everything that sparkles isn't gold. This is a very true statement, and we must be careful that when we accept gifts that we know if they are coming from God, or if they are gifts from Satan with the objective to cause us to damage.

God has given us the freedom of choice; therefore we have the option to accept a gift or not. While it would be foolish to do so, we actually have the option to decline gifts that God offers. He's not going to force us to accept anything; God allows us to choose to accept Him freely, along with all that comes with being a child of a King. We can accept willingly or not. We are under no obligation, so with that in mind we have to discern the gifts that are being offered to us and then decide if the gift is meant for our good or meant for our demise. The Word states: "Every good gift and every perfect gift is from above" (James 1:17) Therefore, it would seem reasonable to think that "every bad gift and every defective gift is from below." If God only gives good gifts, then Satan gives only bad or harmful gifts. If God wants us to have life more abundantly then Satan wants us to live a life that is in a deficit. If God wants to enlarge our territory, then Satan's job is to decrease it. If God desires that we live in prosperity, then Satan's desire is that our lives be in lack...Good Gifts vs. Bad Gifts, God's Gifts vs. Satan's Gifts. God wants us to choose life, while Satan wants our fate to be the same as his will be, death.

As I continue to learn this lesson and strive to be selective in the gifts I accept, I encourage each of you to do the same. Allow the spirit of discernment to work actively in your lives so that we can avoid gag gifts and the hurts that come along with them, and to be able to discern the gifts that truly come from God. The word says that we must try or test all things. We have to work at discerning the

Flowers From The Master's Garden

origin of things that walk into our lives. If we find that a gift doesn't look like it comes from a sender that we recognize, we need to mark it "Return to Sender" and reject it. However, if we are sent a gift from a Giver we do recognize, we can rest assured that it is meant for our good and that it will bring with it the joy that God intends for us.

As far as I'm concerned, I'm done with gag gifts, whoopee cushions, fake throw up, hand buzzers, fake blood, imitation jewels, fake diamonds, fool's gold, and pleather. I am looking for the real gifts, the blessings God has for me. I am at a point where anything less is unacceptable. Why settle for something imitation when God wants to give us the real thing? It's a hard lesson to learn when you've become accustomed to accepting just any old thing, just any ole gift, but here is a lesson that's worth learning. God's gift may not come at the time you want, but one thing is for sure, it's better to wait on the gifts that God wants to bless you with, than settle for the gag gift that Satan wants to throw your way.

Chapter 11

A Specialized Diet Plan

Not long ago I was a part of a conversation where someone was sharing that they had been recently diagnosed with gout. During this conversation she began to share a list of foods that could no longer be a part of her everyday diet, foods that could contribute to the painful flare-ups that come with such a condition. It was amazing how many items from her diet were going to have to be removed from her daily menu planning and intake. After a while of going over all the foods that she COULDN'T eat, the question was finally raised, almost in despair, *"What foods CAN she eat?"* That question shifted the conversation and the focus from what she couldn't have to researching foods that were rich in nutrients that she could have and that would assist in keeping the flare-ups to a minimum.

Later as I thought more on the conversation, God began to deposit something in my spirit. Each of us have things in our lives that from time to time will flare up and cause us to waver in our faith, or to question if our relationship with God is as strong as we think. During these flare ups we can experience feelings of fear, low self-esteem, nervousness, self-doubt, and other feelings that are contrary to what God would have us believe about ourselves. These times of spiritual flare-ups can hold us captive, where we are so focused on our failures and shortcomings that we don't see that there IS something we can do to minimize the number of flare-ups we experience. We need to identify the "foods" that can no longer be a part of our spiritual diets, but more importantly, we need to identify the "foods" that will strengthen us while we're going through our conditions.

For years I battled with how to overcome low self-esteem and feelings of self-doubt. For a long time when I was complimented for any reason, my first thought was not to believe that the person sharing the compliment was being sincere. Why would I think that? For years my spirit was being fed "foods" that were consistently attacking my spiritual health. I heard consistently that I was ugly, fat, a mistake, and that I wasn't good enough to be a wife from my husband at the time. I felt that nothing I did would ever be important, and that my ministry was not as important as someone else's. I also felt that if I left a relationship, nobody would want me, or I would end up as a mistress because nobody would want to marry someone like me. I felt that I had nothing to offer, and I felt that people were lying to me when they said that I was attractive because they pitied me. When you continue to eat and digest "foods" that do not have any nutritional value, your body will become weak, and you will no longer be able to perform at your highest peak. In many cases the body will shut down completely, and you will be unable to perform at all. In the same way as a parent is mindful of the foods that they allow their children to eat, we have to be just as careful of what we allow be digested into our spiritual bodies.

After years of digesting these bad foods, my spiritual immune system had been compromised. I no longer wanted to minister.

When I looked in the mirror all I saw was that ugly woman nobody could possibly love. When I was hurting, I no longer wanted to go to church to receive help from that spiritual dietician. I was sick. I knew I was sick but didn't know how to go about receiving the healing that my spiritual body needed desperately. However, God is a God of grace and mercy, and when we are unable to help ourselves; He becomes our advocate and will conduct a spiritual intervention in our lives by linking us to specialists that have the answers to help us embrace our recovery. While those old symptoms will still try to pop up and suggest that I have not been healed, and although the recovery process was long and hard; God is a healing God and has helped me embrace my healing and deliverance.

During those moments when those old symptoms try to flare up and I have to fight feelings of self-doubt, I have learned that I have to be very mindful of my spiritual diet. I have to feed my spirit foods that are rich in ingredients that will stimulate who I am in Christ; I need foods that stimulate my spiritual immune system to say I am because God is. I need foods that tell my body that I am fearfully and wonderful made, and foods that bring iron to my blood that says I am created in His image. I need foods that strengthen my muscles and tell them that no weapon formed against me shall prosper, and foods that deliver spiritual calcium to my bones that let them know old things are passed away and behold all things arc ncw.

I need foods that will stimulate the dendrites in my body to deliver messages to my brain that say to God I am priceless, and a one-of-a-kind jewel that doesn't have to settle for anything or anyone. I need food that says I am a person of worth and I will always seek another person of worth with whom I can connect. I don't have to accept someone who thinks less of me than what my Heavenly Father thinks of me. These are the foods that I have to feed my body continually. This is a lifelong diet plan. My diet may not be what you need to sustain your body, but this is the diet that will keep ME strong spiritually. Perhaps you're dealing with a health condition; your meal plan may consist of foods that will stimulate your memory on how God healed the woman with an issue of blood (Matthew 9:18-26), or how God restored the sight of the blind man. (John 9). You may need to take a vitamin that will strengthen your heart and remind you that Jesus took stripes upon His back specifically for your healing. (Isaiah 53:5) Maybe your condition is fear; your diet is going to have to consist of foods rich in antioxidants that say God has not given you a spirit of fear, but of love and of power and of a sound mind. (2 Timothy 1:7) You may need to drink plenty of spiritual water that will saturate your body with a spiritual hydrogen oxygen combination to remind you that He will never leave you nor forsake you. (Hebrews 13:5)

Maybe your body is suffering from a finance deficiency; your diet will need to include foods rich in proteins that declare you are not in lack but in abundance. You will need to flush your spiritual kidneys with liquids that remind you that if God takes care of the sparrow how much more will He care for you. (Matthew 6:26) Eat spiritual fruits that tell your body that your Father is rich in houses and lands, and that you have access to all that He has; He desires that you live an abundant life. (John 10:10)

None of us are completely healthy spiritually; all of us have areas of weakness that we have to keep in check continually. In the natural, we take vitamins and other medications that will keep our bodies stable; we have to devote the same amount of care to our spiritual bodies. Just as there are healthy foods and restaurants that cater to healthy living, we also have available to us various foods and resources that will assist us in keep our spiritual bodies strong. The word of God offers an excellent menu, foods that will satisfy any taste bud, even the pickiest eater. Praise and Worship will always flush our bodies and bring us to a place of communion with God. We have no excuse; God has provided what we need to keep ourselves healthy, but we have to take charge of our spiritual health and declare that we are whole in Him.

In my case, there is something very specific I desire to see God do in my life, but I know that because of what I desire to see God do in my life it is easy to feel unworthy; and to feel looked over or ignored. So, to keep those flares at bay or at a minimum, I walk around with my Kurt Carr brand of spiritual vitamin water that says:

".......AND ONE DAY IF I PRAY, I KNOW MY DREAMS WILL COME TO BE............I BELIEVE GOD, HE IS INCREDIBLE, INVINCIBLE, HE CAN CRUMBLE THE IMPOSSIBLE, YES I BELIEVE GOD, AND ALTHOUGH MY FAITH SOMETIMES IS TESTED, ON THIS SHAKY ROAD I TROD, I.....OH I...... BELIEVE GOD!!" (*"I Believe God"* Artist: Kurt Carr Album: Just The Beginning Released: 2008)

Chapter 12

An Exclamatory Imperative

I recall as a girl in grade school I learned about various types of sentences, and how they were used to convey what the speaker or writer was saying. We are living in a time where believers and non-believers are experiencing the most challenging times of their lives. People are searching for answers and are trying to get an understanding of why life is going in the direction that it is. People are desperate to find an end to their situation.

As believers we have inside information to the questions that plague so many people. We know the One who has all power; we are directly linked to the One who can take any situation and turn it around in our favor. In fact, not only do we know who holds the power, but as sons and daughters, we also have been given 100% access to the power. The most powerful weapon against what takes place in each of our lives is the power that is possessed in our tongue. The Word declares that the tongue, this small instrument, holds the power of life and death. Our words have the power to change our situation, and if we as believers would not only learn how to tap into this power but actually learn how to operate it, can you imagine what we could do, and the destruction of strongholds that could take place?

When we think of the word POWER, there is an assumption that comes along with it. Power is a force, and power commands attention. Power lets you know that there is some sort of action taking place or getting ready to take place. Power denotes strength. Power commands authority! So based on that, if we are going to access the power that Christ has given us, there is a certain posture we must have, and there is a certain attitude we must take, if I dare say it, we must exercise a spiritual arrogance when we step up to command this power.

As God was depositing this in me, I recalled what I learned about the different types of sentences that exist. A DECLARATIVE sentence is a sentence that makes a statement; it may be a statement that may not have a lot of authority behind it. "God is." A true statement, but it's a statement that isn't guaranteed to command the attention of the reader. An INTERROGATIVE sentence is a sentence that ask a question, where information is being obtained. "God is?" This is actually a question that no believer should ask because of course He is good, but for our purposes this sentence is asking for information that the writer may not know the answer. The next two types of sentences I'd like to the combine are the EXCLAMATORY sentence and the IMPERATIVE sentence. These two types of sentences command attention. They excite the senses. Both these sentences end with an exclamation point, and they tell the reader that there is serious emotion behind the statement. While the EXCLAMATORY sentence shows strong emotion, the IMPERATIVE sentence takes it to the next level by turning the emotion of the IMPERATIVE sentence into a command. Not only is there strong emotion in what is being said, but the writer wants to reinforce his/her position in what was said. "GOD IS!" The simple change in punctuation changes the entire feel of what the writer or speaker is saying.

We are living in an IMPERATIVELY EXCLAMATORY times. There are things taking place in our lives that need to be commanded, where we do not have the luxury of asking if it can happen, or where are we in the position of taking a laid-back kind of attitude. We have to use the power of our tongue and the power of our words to declare that something is GOING to happen; it is GOING to take place! We have the power to take a situation and completely turn it around in our favor, and it's time to take the power that has been given to us and put it into full operation. I don't know about you, but the situations in my life are calling for full power. I don't need things just to happen. I need a supernatural move of power, so I don't have the luxury of being passive. I have to make some demands; I have to declare some things, and I have to command some things to change. My words have to have an exclamation point behind it. I can't ask if my needs are going to be met; I have to declare with power and authority that MY NEEDS ARE MET! I can't just randomly say that my son will grow up to be a man of God, NO!! In the age in which we live, I have to make a command, MY SON, RAHJON AMIR DAR'RELL STALLWORTH, WILL BE A MAN OF GOD!

I can't say Satan, will you please let my finances go, I have to stand up with authority and say SATAN GET YOURSELF OFF MY FINANCES!! If the Word declares that the tongue is a weapon, then we need to learn how to use the weapon effectively. You don't send a civilian into the heat of a war; he will have no clue how to use his weapon against his adversary. He won't know how to defend himself. It is the same way with our tongue; we have been given a weapon, and it's time that we activate it and call those things that are not as though they were. I AM DEBT FREE! MY CHILDREN ARE

COVERED! MY BODY IS HEALED! MY SPOUSE IS ON THE WAY! MY HOME IS PURCHASED! THAT POSITION IS MINE! GOD WILL NEVER LEAVE ME! I'M BLESSED GOING IN! I'M BLESSED GOING OUT! I'M THE HEAD AND NOT THE TAIL! I AM CHOSEN! I AM FEARFULLY AND WONDERFULLY MADE! I AM A WINNER! I AM AN OVERCOMER! I AM BEAUTIFUL TO GOD!

Once we first learn how to use our weapon and then actually take it out and use it when we're in the thick of battle, then we will see a supernatural move in our lives.

Those things that are plaguing others won't bother us, because we know how to combat them. Whoever heard of a wimpy warrior? Think about David. While David was just a boy, a shepherd, he had more power and courage then those who were actually being sent to fight the battle. The army said this giant is too mighty for us. David was like, what in the world are you talking about? WE are the children of the Most High God! David said: *Look, I have enough confidence in the God I serve to deal with this situation.* He didn't second-guess if he could defeat Goliath.

He wasn't passive; he took authority over the situation and TOLD King Saul, not only would he go up against this giant, but also he WOULD defeat him! His words took command of a situation. While the army was standing around talking in fear, David changed the whole dynamic of the situation by telling not only King Saul, but also the enemy what was GOING to take place. Before he picked up a stone, Goliath, King Saul and the army were well informed of what

WAS going to happen and what the final outcome was GOING to be. There were no surprises on anyone's part!!

Friends, it's time to command our situations and let it be known what IS going to happen in our lives. We need to open up our mouths and declare what is and isn't going to take place. The devil is using everything that is at his disposal. Isn't it about time that we use all that's at our disposal?

Chapter 13

A Lesson In the Cake

Often we hear that we have to go through periods of fire so that God can purify us and cleanse us from things in our lives that are not compatible with Him. Recently I was listening to my long-distance Pastor speak on baking a cake that really impacted me. He shared that when you bake a cake, it is put into the oven as batter, but after the proper time in the oven it comes out as a cake. What an awesome analogy!! As I began to think on this, God began to show me that you have to apply things to your lives where you are in order to help you get through. Nobody wants to think about going into a furnace in order to become what God would have you to be, but who wouldn't mind going into an oven if the end result is coming out as a cake. Who doesn't like cake?? (LOL)

At various times in our lives, God takes us through transformations. He may want to get rid of some things. He may want to add some things. He may want to reveal some things. In all these cases, transformation and change involves some sort of heat process. Gold has to be heated for it to be transformed into a valuable mineral. Heat has to be applied to clay for it to be formed into a pot. An iron or steamer has to be applied to our clothes to get the wrinkles out, and heat has to be applied to our hair for it to come out straight and silky. Usually, when transforming is involved, heat of some kind is used. So instead of complaining about the heat, we need to change our way of thinking; and instead of looking at the heat, we need to look at the end result. We may not like to iron, but the outcome is crisp clothes. We may not like to sit under the hair dryer for hours, but the end result is sassy looking hair. We may not want to wait for the cake to come out of the oven, but the outcome is a sweet dessert. Heat ensures that we don't look the way we went in; heat says that you will be different when the process ends. You can't go through a heated situation and come out the same as when you went in. It is impossible.

Heat and time are the tools for transformation. You can't put a cake in the oven and let it stay there for 5 minutes and expect cake. You can't put your clothes in the dryer for a few seconds and expect them to be ready to wear; and you can't sit under the hair dryer for 2 minutes and expect your hair to look fabulous. Time is involved, and if the time is discontinued the outcome is not going to be what was intended.

I love Red Velvet Cake with cream cheese frosting, so I have declared that I am a spiritual Red Velvet Cake. I may not like the heat that is going on in my life right now. I get frustrated; I'm uncomfortable. I cry, I hurt, and I've screamed on occasion; but at the end of the day, I know that is my end result. Once we have gone through the heat and the transformation that needs to take place, God will reward me for my patience and endurance. He'll add something sweet and beautiful to my life, like spiritual frosting. Jesus Himself experienced the heat of His calling, so he understands that heat isn't comfortable.

He knows, He sympathizes, and He will not let the trying of heat in our lives to go unrecognized.

The song says, "When God gets through with me, I shall come forth as pure gold." (*"Please Be Patient With Me"*, James Cleveland/ Albertina Walker, Savory Records, 1979) Let's change that a bit: "When God gets through with me, I shall come forth as sweet cake." I love gold, but again, who doesn't love cake?? It's all in how you look at it.

Chapter 14

A Daddy's Love

Some time ago I heard the Lord speak an awesome word in the midst of a father's hurt and concern for his daughter. We know God to be so many things: helper, healer, provider, protector, Almighty, Ruler, and many more things…but do we know Him as Daddy? The word "Daddy" sets a special tone. It speaks to the relationship you have with your father. Father or even Dad tends to be more formal, an acknowledgment of someone's title, role or position.

They say that George Washington was the father of our country, a title that deserved respect, but not intimacy. Those who remember Daddy Grace, that name testified to the nature of his relationship with those who followed him. There is an intimacy, an untouchable place in the hearts of both the child and the father, and when the child goes from saying Dad to Daddy, it sets the tone and the atmosphere. The word Daddy says that there is a naked trust between father and child.

Years ago, I was sexually assaulted. I was young, and because of my age there were questions about what had happened. I could not answer them because I didn't have knowledge or experience in that area at that time. I will always remember how my dad took on the role of caring for me during that time - the hospital visits, the conversations with the police, the conversations we had when medically speaking. Was there a chance I would have gotten pregnant? All those things were so intimate that the title dad does not fit the role he played in my life. Then and now, 30+ years after the assault, Elder Ronald A. Jenkins is still Daddy to me. He proved himself not only to be my father, but my Daddy.

The title of Daddy is bestowed upon someone who has earned that position. There are lots of fathers, but how many children feel the intimacy in the relationship to call them Daddy? A Daddy is who you call when you're in trouble, but a Daddy is also who you may try to avoid if you know your actions may call for correction. A child doesn't walk up to any male and start calling him Daddy; that relationship is reserved for the person who shows the characteristics of a Daddy. Even children who don't see their fathers often develop a Daddy image in their minds of who they think their father is or who they want him to be. My son is a perfect example of that. No matter what may happen, his father will always be Daddy. His heart wants his Daddy, and no matter what Daddy does or doesn't do, nothing can take the image he has created of his father away from him. (Side bar: this is the reason why as mothers we should NEVER speak against the fathers of our children, no matter what he does or doesn't do. It is never our job to plant negative seeds in the lives of our children as it relates to their fathers. I know it can be hard, trust me I know, but at the end of the day, our children do not need our help to define what kind of fathers they have. As they get older they will learn for themselves, and, as I am learning even now, God can turn any situation around for the good. A father who has not taken his position as father seriously or who has neglected his position all together, with God's intervention, can become a whole new man.)

Recently a co-worker of mine met her father for the first time; my co-worker is 49 years old!! For years she has talked about wanting to meet her father. For the 10 years I have known and worked with her, the craving for her Daddy was dominant in her life; now after 49 years she was finally blessed with the opportunity to meet him a few weeks ago. At 49 all she talks about is her Daddy…her Daddy said, her Daddy did, her Daddy called, her Daddy gave…. it's all about her Daddy. The need for a Daddy never left her, and now that he's in her life she is like a child whose Daddy has come home after a business trip or a long military deployment, she's excited, she's renewed, and her self-esteem has soared!!! Daddy has come home!!

How much more does our Heavenly Father want to hold the position of Daddy in our lives? He wants to have that intimate, special relationship that exists between a parent and child. He wants us to cry Daddy when we hurt. He wants us to come to Him as Daddy when we need something, and He wants us to turn to Him as Daddy when we're in trouble. He's Daddy, and it's His honor to come to us when we call. Just like in the case of a daughter, no matter how old she gets, her natural Daddy will always be wrapped around her little finger; we have our Daddy wrapped around our fingers, and at the faintest cry for Daddy His heart strings are pulled and He responds.

So, the question today is this: are we really Daddy's little girl, or Daddy's little man? Do we have the type of relationship with our Father that allows us to even call Him Daddy? Do we have a relationship where when we cry "Daddy" He comes running? When the devil is attacking us, do we have a relationship where the devil scatters when we say I'm gonna tell my Daddy on you? When we are hurt, can we cry on Daddy's shoulder? Will Daddy hold us and rock us and assure us that everything will be alright? Can we call Daddy at any time of the day or night and know that He's gonna respond and respond quickly? Does Daddy talk to us and share His desires for our lives? Does Daddy make sure we have everything we need and then because He loves us so very much gives us even some of the "toys" we desire?

If we cannot call our Father Daddy, then it is time that we strengthen that relationship bond and get to the place where not only is He Father, but where He is Daddy. Not only does He have a special place in our hearts, but where we have a special place in His. It's about an intimate relationship. Prince Charles will be the king of England one day, and to the world he is father to two sons, but at the end of the day, when the duties of his position end, he is Daddy to William and Henry. It was Daddy, who helped them mourn the death of their mother; and it's Daddy who helps them manage their very public lives - not the father of Prince William or Prince Henry, but the man they call Daddy. It's the same with us. He is our King, our Lord, Our El Shaddai, and Our Jehovah Rophe.... but when we are in our quiet time, can we also say He is our Daddy.

Chapter 15

A Lesson In My Mom's Flower Garden

Those who knew my Mom, Evang. Mildred Jenkins, know how much she loved flowers. My mom would spend hours planting, weeding, fertilizing, and doing all those things that would produce beautiful flower gardens. Mom would spend a lot of time at a local nursery and in flower brochures picking out flowers and learning the best conditions to make them thrive in her own garden. My sister Tara and I had the awful task of watering these lovely gems and making sure that the gardens were free of weeds.

As a person who was and still is not the most outdoors kind of person, this was a chore I detested!! While I liked how pretty they were, I could never understand why I had to spend so much time in a garden that I never wanted, they weren't my flowers, and they weren't the pride and joy of my life but my Mom's. However, godly wisdom told me not to voice such thoughts knowing well that such expressions could lead to the various applications to my hind parts (lol), so year after year Tara and I would make sure our gardening chores were done to the best of our ability.

One flower my Mom loved in particular was the tulip. They had such bright colors and came in a variety of shapes and sizes, and this was the perfect flower for the garden that set off the front of our house. In studying the care of tulips, Mom learned that there are tulip bulbs you can plant that are called "Annuals." Annuals are flowers you plant one time and they come up and bloom one time. Then there are plants called "Perennials;" these are plants that you plant one time but they come up year after year.

In the "flower garden" of life I am learning that there are two types of flowers that adore our garden. There are "flowers," people and situations that God has placed in our lives to be a blessing to us over and over. These "Perennials" can be a spouse, children, mentors, a Pastor, the church we attend or anything that God sees fit to keep in our lives and that will add to the beauty of our "garden." Then there are "Annual" flowers, flowers that bloom one time, for a particular season, and that's it. "Annuals" may be there for a particular purpose that only God knows and sees. They are there to teach you lessons and help you to prepare and progress to the next level in God.

One particular year, I recall my Mom buying these tulip bulbs that when they bloomed were going to be a beautiful shade of purple (Mom's favorite color was purple). My Mom planted these tulip bulbs thinking they were Perennials, and that they would come back year after year, in reality however, they were Annuals and bloomed only for one season. When they didn't sprout up the following year, my Mom who kept all her plant care labels, looked back to find that what she had purchased were bulbs that only bloomed once in the spring instead of bulbs that would come back year after year.

Sometimes we may think that a particular "flower" is meant to be in our lives to stay, when in reality they are only supposed to be there for a season. No matter how much we may want the "flower" to keep blossoming, it is not meant to be a permanent part of our "garden." It's there to give its beauty for a time and then it is meant to fade. Another side to this coin is that the "flower" we planted may be a mistake all around. The same way my Mom purchased the wrong type of tulip bulb, Annual versus a Perennial, sometimes we plant things in our lives that are not meant to be there at all; we make errors. Some errors fade in time, but some errors become a part of our life's "flower garden" that we will continually have to handle. Some of the results of our planting may result in a situation such as a child who is NEVER (and I repeat NEVER) considered a mistake, but just the same it is a flower that is a permanent part of our garden. Although it is beautiful, there are still challenges that may be a part of planting a "flower bulb" that may not have been a part of God's original "landscaping" plans for us. Other plants that may come up may be illnesses that we can't get rid of, mental and physical challenges, debt, loss of possessions, things and situations that we may never be able to get back or recover from.

I have a good friend who was brought up in the "Family Business." He worked hard for years, learned the ins and outs, and everything there was to know. He even went to school to obtain the certifications. When it became time for him to take over, a series of events cut him out and the business went to another. Hurt and destroyed by what had taken place, my friend gathered himself up and opted to start his own business, which in a short period of time has flourished into a business that is beyond any business of the same type in his area.

Here is what can we glean from this story. My friend sowed into the "family garden" thinking that he was planting "Perennials," something that would last his lifetime and that he would be able to pass down to his children. However, the reality of it is that God's actual plan was that the "family garden" be filled with "Annuals", flowers that were only for a season. While my friend may have desired to plant something that would have been longer term, and yes that was and is God's intention for him, the key was that God never intended him to plant in the "Family Garden." God wanted more for my friend. God wanted him to relocate to a different area of "land" and plant a new garden, a better garden, and if the truth be told, the "new garden" is far better than the original garden, and the harvest that is coming forth is more bountiful then I'm sure my friend even anticipated.

Yes, there is a lot of hard work that goes into developing new "landscaping," but the rewards that are now being seen show us that God has the final say. He, and He alone knows what type of seeds to plant, why they must be planted, as well as where and when they should be planted. Sometimes things come to destroy the flowers that we plant, but one thing is for sure, if God intends for us to have Perennials in our lives, Perennials we shall have, as in the example of my friend.

In my experience, I have learned that we must be very mindful of what type of "flowers" we grow in our "gardens;" first, we need to be very particular regarding what type of seeds we plant, and we must make sure those are the seeds not only we want to grow, but that God wants us to grow in our "garden." We must also recognize if the plants we sow are the plants that should be a part of our permanent "landscaping" plans, or are they're plants that will only bloom for a short time, if at all.

From watching my Mom for many years, I walked away with the conclusion that gardening is not an easy task; it takes constant care and diligence if you desire it to produce an abundant harvest. I have also come to the conclusion, that in the natural, while I may love flowers, I did not inherit the green thumb my Mom had. (Now my sister Tara, on the other hand, may be another story.) I am more of a flower in the vase kind of gal, grateful for the hard work that others have put in which allow me the honor of being able to purchase them and have them adorn my home.

If I am ever blessed with a home where I am able to actually plant flowers, I may plant a few purple Tulips for the sake of my Mom's memory, but after that I'm a Marigold kinda gurl, a flower where the seeds come in an envelope, sprinkle them, cover them, water them, save the dried flower after it's died and plant more the following year.

But in the "Flower Garden" of my life, I need to be a diligent gardener. I need to make sure that I plant the right seeds, and make sure that the soil is in the best condition for planting and make sure that before weeds take over the loveliness of the flowers that I get in there and pluck them out!!

It's amazing how God can take a simple concept and expand in a way that you have a lesson you can refer to over and over again. Who knew that the years I spent hating all the work that was put into weeding my Mom's garden and watching her develop it would lead to a life-changing lesson 20+ years later.

Chapter 16

A Lesson In True Love

True love....

When you already KNOW from the beginning that someone is gonna mess up, hurt you, betray you, talk about you, deny you, make you mourn and YET, despite having all that information beforehand, you STILL love them!! Mmmmm!! Now when you check that kind of love that Christ gives to us against the type of love we show others, do we really and truly love? My desire is to love people, no matter what happens.

I am embracing the fact that people ARE going to hurt me sometimes, that they WILL betray me every once in a while, WILL stir up my anger, MAY make me cry, but these are things I that know will happen. People aren't perfect and are subject to error, so because I know this, my desire is to look beyond human error and still love unconditionally. It will not always be easy, but Christ has set the standard. How can we not love people who we know will mess up, when on the flip side of the coin, at some point in time we are going to do the very same things to someone else? I'm blessed that after several years, God helped me to let my past go, and forgive those who hurt me. It was literally a long, uphill journey, but how God did it for me a while back was awesome (that's for another day).

One thing that God also showed me was that many marriages could be saved if people would go into it knowing that at some point their spouse will hurt or disappoint them. If they prepare for that, then they will be able to operate in the love that Christ intends for our marriages. God has already let us know that we all have mess to handle. Once I know and embrace the fact that neither me nor my spouse are perfect, then we can love them same way that Christ loves us - unconditionally. If we accept that, then we won't be hurt so easily and disappointed by the one whom God sends to us.

Chapter 17

The Emergency Broadcast System

All of us can recall a time when in the middle of our favorite show, right before the big reveal, there was a station interruption!! When I was growing up in the Boston area, the announcer would come across with something very close to this: "This is a test of the Emergency Broadcast Systems. The broadcasters in your area, in voluntary cooperation with local officials, have developed this test to keep you informed in case of an emergency. If this HAD been an actual emergency, you would have been advised of news and information pertaining to your local area.

This concludes the test of the Emergency Broadcast Systems." Friends, yesterday was ONLY a test; there was no real emergency, and you did not have to run for cover!! Every so often spiritual tests have to come to our "area" so that we know how to perform in the event of a life- threatening, all out devil attack should arise. HOWEVER - REJOICE!! It's a new day; yesterday was a ONLY a test.

Now you can go back to your "regularly scheduled program that was already in progress!!" (LOL) Much like the fire and bomb drills all of us experienced in school, it's not a real fire; you just have to go through the process of preparing for a fire or emergency so that if there is ever a real fire or threat, you won't freak out, but will seek God's direction on how to function in a danger situation. Single file, walking in a spiritually-minded, orderly fashion to the place of safety!! BE ENCOURAGED EVERYONE … THIS IS ONLY A TEST!!!

Chapter 18

A Single's Gift

Recently I was reading a post of a good friend who was sharing his thoughts on being single, and the labels that can be attached to being single. Often as a single, others tend to ask why you are single, and will assume that the reasons are negative... You can't get anybody, or they assume that you are miserable, or they may feel that you're too damaged, too old or set in your ways. They may assume that you are desperately lonely, depressed, or have a void or thirst that cannot be quenched. For some, these assumptions may be true. Too often, people feel a sense of yearning because they are single, and that yearning can lead to depression and other negative attributes. All of these scenarios may lead singles into doing things that make them seem desperate.

However, if the single person has committed himself or herself to Christ, then being single does not hold the same characteristics as it does for the world. While you may not want to be single, and at times experience feelings that come with wanting to share your life with someone special, the distress that the world feels and the titles that they place on someone single does not have to be titles we have to own.

In the last several years of being unattached, God has taught me some wonderful things. God taught me one of these jewels as I was thinking about my friend's post. God let me know that if you marry someone just because you are lonely, or because people have condemned you for being single, and you carry yourself as such, in reality you have nothing to offer a spouse because you are not at a place where you have anything to give but brokenness. Instead of being able to come to the table with all the beautiful things that Christ has developed and deposited in you, you come to the table with what you feel you have lacked.

You don't come to the table with what you have built; but instead you come with what, in your opinion, was broken. At the same time, if you come to the marriage table content and excited about the things that God has done in and through your life while in your single season, you will come with something to offer and with something to share. That doesn't mean you have to like being single; it just means that while you are waiting for God to bless you, you are building wealth that you later will be able to share with that someone whom God is preparing to share their lives with you.

Long ago, if you were planning to marry, the woman would have a "Hope Chest" that was started by the bride's mother or a close female family member. This Hope Chest often contained heirlooms, handmade quilts, family china, a broach, a wedding dress passed down, and other tokens of love for a bride to create a home. These items could be of high financial value or items that were sentimental and precious. In the spirit it is the same way, while we are single, we are building up treasure, a spiritual dowry. Treasures and lessons based on the experiences of life, as well as treasures that only God can deposit into us.

These treasures will not only benefit us during our single season, but they will also bless the person whom God, in the proper season, will send to us. God knows what each of us needs and prepares us for that which is ahead of us. God knows what I need, but he also knows what the person I will be connected to needs. As I walk in this season of singleness, He is depositing things within me that not only benefit my current life, but He is depositing into me treasures, a rich dowry that I will be able to share with the spouse yet to come. God will allow me to come to the table with something spiritually rich to offer the one He's keeping for me.

I have known and have been acquainted with people who are determined to remain single because they want to prove a point. They want to prove that they don't need to be married to be happy. They don't need a special connection, and because of this, they fight against a gift that God wants to use as a blessing for them. There are seasons, even when married, that God wants people to enjoy time alone where He can share time with them; where He can refresh, and deposit into them, and where they can commune with Him. But then there are seasons when God gives a gift to deposit into someone's life; a special gift that is designed for a specially chosen person.

This gift is not for everyone, but for someone that has been selected just for you. It's a treasure that only you can give. On the flipside, there are gifts and treasures that God wants to bless you with; gifts that have been designed just for you that only someone who's been created especially and exclusively for you can deposit into you. There are things that God wants you to have that are just for you alone, and because of that He wraps it in a special person, one special person, and presents him/her to you. It's all about seasons and the changing of seasons in our lives. Why would you reject what God may want to bless you with, or hold on to things He has blessed you with, that He wants you to give to someone exclusively? And on the flip side, why would you want to walk into something empty-handed? Why would you want to come to the table with nothing to offer or before it's ready to be given?

If you desire to be married, then your season of singleness is the time to glean all that Christ has for you, while remembering that it's not all about us, but it's also about the gifts in us that Christ wants us to share with that special person. Once God has blessed you, allow Him to bless you with someone who not only you can pour into them what God has given you, but allow Him to bless you and give you someone in whom He has also given special gifts to pour into you.

As my friend said so eloquently, singleness doesn't mean that you have to accept the titles the world has associated with being single. You can enjoy this time and glean all that God has for you spiritually as well as naturally. When God desires for you to share the wealth of riches He has placed in you with someone special; or just because He loves you so much and wants to fill you with riches through a spouse, then that's the time to thank Him for all that He's allowed you to receive and allow Him to use you in a different capacity. Give yourself time to RECEIVE the gift He wants so much to GIVE YOU and BE a GIFT to someone special.

In nature, God has designed certain things to take place during certain seasons. There is a time to plant, but after the planting, there is a germination period - a time when the seeds get deep in the soil and the roots have an opportunity to become grounded, strong and firm. Come spring, those seeds begin to grow, and in summer they are at the peak of their growth cycle so that when fall comes, they are ready to be harvested and used for that which they were intended.

It is the same in our lives; singleness is a time to have seeds planted in us, for the seeds to take root, and germinate, and when they are at the peak if their growth cycle, they are ready to be shared and used for the nourishment of the one whom God has chosen for our lives. It's exciting to know that while we are waiting for whomever God has for us, that if we stay in tune with Him, He will give us things that will not only bless our lives, but that will bless the life of the gift He intends to give us. My desire is to be at the peak of perfection for the one whom God has for me, and for his fruit to be at peak quality for depositing into my life. So, if he is enjoying this season of singleness now, that is wonderful because that just means that God is depositing things in him that he will be able to present at the marriage table when the season of harvest comes. And likewise, all the things that God is currently depositing into me and allowing me to learn is preparing me to come to the table with a gift that is worthy of the priest whom God has for me.

I have said time and time again, and I really do believe this wholeheartedly; we have to see things with the eyes of discernment, and allow God to show us those things that pertain to our lives, the things that can only be seen through the eyes of Christ.

Chapter 19

A Clear Connection

When I was a child, my Dad would often open and close the church we attended. Although we lived 30-40 minutes outside of Boston, we would be the last people to leave the church every night. While this could be very frustrating to my sister and me while growing up, there was one night of the week that I didn't mind coming home late. Wednesday evening was prayer meeting night, and while I wasn't eager to pray back then, on the way home there was an old-fashioned radio program called The Macomb Mystery Theater.

I would always hear my parents talk about how they would gather around the radio to listen to various studio productions as children that would allow the listener to use their imagination to produce the scenes that were being heard. This Mystery Theater was my chance to do just that. The show was produced out of a Boston radio station, so as long as we were close to the city the signal was clear. Many Wednesday evenings I would sit in the back seat listening to the murder mysteries that were produced while enjoying the various characters and anticipating how the murder would be solved in only 30 minutes. Most nights I would be able to hear the story all the way through, however on days when the weather was less then clear the radio signal would get fuzzy the further away from the city we were, so by the time we would reach Newton, or Newton Heights, often the signal was so weak that my Dad would have to fiddle with the dial to see if he could get the signal to come in strong enough to hear the conclusion of the story. Sometimes his fiddling worked, other times the signal was just too weak, and I was forced to make up my own conclusions to the story.

How many of us are like those old radios, where we are so far from God that the reception is so weak that we can hardly hear what God is saying to us? We have to fiddle with our spiritual dials just to hear the faint sound of His voice. Friends, it's time that we return to the source of our power. How can we hear from God if we are so far away from the spiritual transmission signal? Our relationship with God should be so strong that we don't have to fiddle with dials, and where we don't have to strain our ears to hear from Him. We should be so close to God that whatever He is trying to deposit into us is abundantly clear.

Last week I had the honor of being able to serve as a co- teacher for my church's Vacation Bible School session. The theme this year was "GLOW AND GO," where we talked about the importance of being the light of the world. In one visual demonstration, we had a lamp, where although it was plugged in and the switch turned on, the light would not shine. As students investigated the lamp to see what the problem was, it was discovered that while the lamp WAS plugged in, and WAS turned on, the light bulb was not securely screwed into the socket. Often that how we as children of God are; we go to church, we sing in the choir, we go to Bible study, we participate in all the church activities, but we are not securely connected to the source of the power. Our connection to God is flickering because it is not strong. We seem to do all the right things, but our relationship with God is in need of work. The only way to have a strong connection with God is to develop a relationship with Him, but a relationship cannot be achieved unless personal time is spent with Him.

Have you ever been in a relationship where it seems like the spark has gone out? You may be dating or married, but it seems like you are just going through the motions? Why does this happen? It's because the bond of the relationship hasn't been nurtured; it hasn't been fed, and the next thing you know, before you even realize it, the relationship is weak. People are together but have grown apart. People are living in the same house, but are living separate lives. The phone calls stop, and the date nights cease. At some point, if actions are not taken to revive the relationship, it will die and lives will be forever shattered and changed. You cannot have a strong relationship if you are not committed to seek ways to maintain it by looking for new things in your partner, and by finding ways to keep the relationship exciting.

Our relationship with God is no different; we have to pursue God. We must discover what He likes, what He desires for and from us. We must want to know His will and plan for our lives. As it is when two people are dating, where they seek to know each other is how it should be with our pursuit to know God. Relationships cannot be one-sided if they are to survive. A person cannot pursue someone and not get the same attention in return. It is spiritually selfish for us to expect God to pursue us continually and aggressively, and we do not do the same in return.

The difference in us and with God is that no matter what, God will always actively go after us, and he will actively always want to spend time with us no matter what we do. With us, after a while if someone is trying to pursue someone and is getting no response, that person will say forget it, and determine that the person is not worth the effort. On the other hand, God will never say we are not worth His effort. He will never throw up His hands and say forget it, it's just not worth it. No matter how far we stray, God will always pursue us. Unlike people, God will never stop seeking to make us His own. How many of us have someone in our lives who we can honestly say that they are worth pursuing? How many of us would wait years for that special someone? How many of us believe that he/she is worth so much that we would wait for them, watching them as they perhaps give their love and attention to someone else?

Will we allow ourselves to be hurt, or allow ourselves to ache and yearn while they give their attention to someone who we know will never love them as much as we would? Yet, because we love them that much, and because we value them that much, we wait and we would pursue them subtly, with the hopes that through a miracle their light bulb will illuminate, and they will see us and all the love we are willing and desire to give them.

God is no different; He watches as we stray, and spend time with other lovers. He watches as we hold hands with Him yet when something or someone who seemingly is more exciting comes along we quickly divert our attention, still holding His hand, but our eyes are looking in another direction rather than being focused on the love that we already have. Imagine how you would feel if you were walking hand in hand with that special person and someone of the opposite sex walked by and while still holding your hand, he/she stopped paying attention to you and focused his/her attention on that other person. Imagine how hurt you would feel. Now ask yourself the question: How many times have you been holding God's hand, who has loved you through all your mess, cared for you when you were sick, and who supported you financially and emotionally, given you "just because" gifts, but when something seemly more appealing comes along we turn our heads. How many times have we hurt God, a God who would never in a million years do anything even remotely similar to us? Friends, it is no different than how we would feel if the one we loved so desperately, did the very same thing to us.

It's time to reconnect; it's time to connect our spiritual light bulb back into our Source, it's time to fine-tune that radio so that we can have a strong signal. It's time to reaffirm our "marriage vows," it's time to re-establish our love relationship with God. If a relationship becomes weak, there is always that chance you will never be able to get back what you once had. If you are waiting for that special someone to notice you, there is always the chance that it may never happen; but with God, that is never the case. No matter how far we stray, He is always waiting for us. If our relationship with Him becomes weak, He is always willing to take us back and allow us to re-establish ourselves with Him. God is here. God is always here. His arms are always open. He never walked away. He never got distracted. So now it's up to us to find our way back where we know we belong. Just like when you know you messed up in a relationship, or when you know you should be with someone specific and didn't want to admit it, but you know where you should be, when it's just a matter of obtaining the inner strength to tell that person you want and need them; it's the same with God.

Father I love You. Father I need You. Father I know I don't deserve it, but please grant me Your grace and mercy, and take me back.

Chapter 20

Fashionable Wolves

Wolves can fit into any outfit - from the clergy robe to the postal worker's shorts; from the First Lady's hat to the waitress' skirt. So when dealing with people we need to look and see if there are any wolf-like parts hanging out.

Even Little Red Riding Hood recognized that something was strange about "Grandma." She knew that Grandma didn't have big ears, big eyes, a big nose and big teeth!! She discerned that something was not right about Grandma!! If Little Red Riding Hood discerned that the devil had taken over Grandma and didn't have the spirit of God in her, seems to me that we who do have the Spirit need to do a better job at discerning the devil in wolves' clothing that pop up in our lives trying to act as sheep!!!

Chapter 21

A Policy Disclaimer

How many of you have seen an advertisement for a product or service on TV only for them to have a huge disclaimer at the bottom of the screen that nobody could possibly read? Or perhaps you are taking medication and on your information sheet there is a long list of disclaimer information that lets you know all the side effects that may be associated with taking that particular drug. The devil often offers us things that seem wonderful, but way down at the bottom of the spiritual screen or document, there is a disclaimer that what he is offering may cause you death. Christ, on the other hand, is always up front with what He offers us, and He tells us what may happen if we choose an avenue different from what He has advised.

Let's review the story of Adam and Eve in the Garden of Eden. God was very clear; He let them know that if they ate of the tree of the knowledge of good and evil then they would surely die. There was no misunderstanding; the disclaimer was in bold print. There was nothing sneaky and no tricky wording. If they opted to eat of that tree, they would die, point blank. Now here comes along that shady "lawyer;" he tells Eve, *'If you eat of the tree you will not die, but in fact you will be like God.'* (Genesis 2:17) However, at the bottom of the document was a disclaimer in tiny print saying *'While you will have knowledge you didn't have before, you will be disconnected from the Creator. You will have to work, your children will be born in pain, you will lose your garden privileges, and your life will no longer be the same.'*

Now had Satan been just as up front with Eve as Christ was, her choice would have been different, but by leaving out those important details, Satan's offer seemed more attractive than what God had spoken to them. As a result, from the moment they bit into the fruit, life, as they knew it, was changed forever. Satan comes to deceive; there will never be a time when he will fully disclose the outcome of choosing his options.

You will never get the full picture of what is behind Satan's motives. He works undercover, and he is a master at telling only bits of information. He is quick to merge a lie and a piece of the truth together to make you believe that you have all the information to make and an educated decision, but the truth is that we cannot believe anything that Satan says to us. If we had known that the fine woman we were eyeing was a gold digger, or that sexy brotha we were talking to had us as just one of many women he was dealing with, would we have made the choice to still continue down that path?? Of course not, but Satan does not operate that way; he shows you bits and pieces, enough to get you into a situation that may take years to get out.

The Assistant Pastor at my church often makes a statement along these lines; If you want to go to hell, that is your choice, but before you make that decision, be well informed; have all the information available. Every time he makes that statement, I find it awesome, but it is so true. If you choose to go to hell, that's fine, it's your choice. God is not going to take away your freedom of choice, but if that's what you are determined to do, at least be well informed of what that means. Weigh your options and see if there is a better eternal alternative for you. Make sure you read that fine print at the bottom of all the forms to see if you are willing to accept the terms of Satan's contract.

God doesn't have any hidden agendas, undisclosed information, or print so small where it takes bifocals plus a magnifying glass to read. God is open; His information is laid out on the table and in a language that anyone who truly interested can read and understand. God's contract is in large bold print. He clearly tells us that He will never deceive us. There is no hidden agenda, no secret information, and no hidden cost. He is what He is; His policy is what it is. God is as straightforward as you're going to get. When you opt to connect your life to Christ, and because His desire is to give us life and life more abundantly, He discloses every piece of information available. There is no reason why we would opt to make another choice. He lets you know that He wants to enlarge our territory, and that He desires to give us good gifts. He wants us to prosper, that He wants to give us the desires of our hearts. He wants us to be joint heirs with Him, and He wants us to live and not die.

He tells us that we have access to Him 24 hours a day. He tells us that if we look for Him, we will find Him. He tells us that if we knock, He will open the door. He lets us know that He desires us to be the head and not the tail. He lets us know that in our policy He has given us the power to command mountains to move, and the power to change our circumstances. He gives us the power to call the things that are not yet as if they already exist. God lays out His intentions toward us; He wants us to know that He loves us so much that our policy was signed with His blood. Satan cannot make such disclaimers, and he can't make promises to us that will stand. His policy cannot begin to compare to the policy of Christ, and at the end of the day, when storms come our way, Satan's policy will become ineffective; it will not be able to cover us. God's policy has a 100% coverage guarantee.

Knowing that Satan's whole objective is to make us fall, and that the only intention of Christ is to give us life, then why would you choose to sign Satan's policy when you know that there are aspects of his offer that are either hidden or straight-out lies? You are blessed with the option to choose, to obtain all the information that is available to you, to if you will shop around and examine the fine print of Satan's plan, and then read in full the policy that Jesus offers. With all this information at your fingertips, why would you choose Satan's plan that gives you nothing, but calls for high premiums, and reject God's plan that offers you everything, and it's 100% free?? Maybe it's me. Someone PLEASE help me understand.

Chapter 22

Tunnel Vision

A few weeks ago, I had an experience that reminded me that regardless of what goes on around me, I have to keep my eyes focused on the vision that God has placed in front of me. No matter what is said, no matter what the circumstances look like, I must stay focused on what Christ said to me. I must have spiritual tunnel vision.

Sometimes when God gives us a Word, or places something in our spirit, a situation will come that will make us waver and doubt what we know God has spoken. Sometimes it may be the devil trying to get us off-track, but sometimes the Lord will allow things to take place that will test our faith to see whether we believe God, or if we are putting our trust in what things looks like; or if we trust what others say even if it's different from what God has spoken.

If you know God has said something, you have to believe it. You have to rest in it; you have to have tunnel vision. You can't afford to lose sight of the vision by looking at the scenery around you. Your eyes have to be focused on what is straight ahead. What is in front of you is better than the sights that are along the way. Our walk cannot be a sightseeing tour. We have to block those things that glitter on either side of us and focus on what is straight ahead.

What is going on around you, and it does not matter what others say. All that matters is the Word that GOD has spoken, what GOD has shown you, and what GOD has deposited into your spirit!!!

I have fallen in love with the song by Kurt Carr that says, "I BELIEVE GOD."(Kurt Carr, Album: Just The Beginning, 2008) Tunnel vision means that we have to say to ourselves continually, "I believe God." Tunnel vision will ask, *'Whose report do you believe? Is there anything too hard for God? Can these dry bones live?'* Tunnel vision does not allow you to look to the left or to the right, because your eyes are focused on the prize.

I encourage those who have received a word from God, and who has a God-given vision in their spirit to keep your spiritual eyes focused on what God has said. Don't allow what people say, or what situations look like to defer you from what God has said. If God said it, believe!, If God said it, it has to come to pass. God is not a man that He should lie; He will not allow His Word to return to Him void. This means once God says it, it's as good as done.

Chapter 23

A Divine Gift... No Imitations

Think back in your mind about the most precious natural gift someone has given you. Perhaps it was a family heirloom that someone had passed down, or a sentiment gift that was given to you by your child, or maybe a special friend or spouse gave you something they really couldn't afford but simply wanted you to have. These gifts are precious to us not just because of the gift itself, but because of the heart that accompanied the gift.

God has DIVINE gifts for each of us; these gifts can only be given to us by God. Divine gifts can be both natural and spiritual, but they are gifts that are designed especially for you.

Let's go back to those gifts that are precious to us. How do we treat those gifts? Sometimes we take them out only for special occasions or for special guests; sometimes we don't take them out at all and just leave them in the box or case. Some we display for others to view and enjoy, but in every case we have to agree that those gifts are handled and treated with a certain amount of respect. Not everyone gets to touch them. You don't take them out for just anyone, and if they break, more often than not they cannot be replaced.

When God blesses us with a spouse, it's a one-of-a-kind special gift; it's tailored specially for you, based on what you need, want and desire. There is a saying that says you have to kiss a lot of frogs before you find your prince, but when you allow God to give you a gift, while there is some care involved in making sure that gift continues to sparkle, no other gift will even begin to compare.

Recently a very good friend of mine shared that he has found the woman who was intended for him; his DIVINE GIFT has been revealed to him. As I watched and listened to him, I saw how he has really embraced this woman as a God-given gift. When you realize that God has given you something precious, your attitude towards the gift is different than any other gift you have or may receive in the future.

You treat it with respect, you're protective of it, you're concerned about it, you want to make sure that no harm comes to it, you place it on a pedestal to keep it safe, you love it, you cherish it, you pray for it, you cover it, and you shield it. You're not afraid or ashamed to share how precious the gift is, and there is nothing that will drive you away from your gift. You have the understanding that the gift has been DIVINELY directed. It doesn't matter if you are male or female; the one thing that is clear is that with so many relationships failing, God has entrusted you with something precious and you should treat it as DIVINE.

So, what are the lessons? Don't settle for imitation gifts. Make sure that your gift has been DIVINELY given, and do not accept cheap replicas. The same way you can buy an imitation Gucci bag, the devil has impostors and imitations that looks like they're divine, sound divine, speak divinely, and even may for a moment treat you divinely, but in reality it is a cheap replica that with the test of time will crumble. Wait for your DIVINE gift. While you may not know how, when or where he or she may be presented to you, rest assured that waiting for you is a DIVINE gift that God will present to you, and it's intended only for you.

Chapter 24

No Big Deal? Really?!

God is such a loving God that often He will show Himself to save us from ourselves, which is Grace and Mercy in true effect.

Early this morning I experienced God's desire to see me make it across the finish line. Sometimes it's not the huge things that cause us to stumble, lose focus, or waver; it's those little, insignificant things that for a quick moment may distract us, but may cause us to lose out on the things that God wants to bless us with, those things that we've been praying for.

God knows just how to speak to us and just how to get our attention. For me, an unexpected text message at an unexpected time today, a time of day when normally I would have been in a deep sleep, reminded me that if I'm serious about God and serious about being the type of woman that God can brag on and depend on, then I have to keep both my spiritual and natural eyes focused straight ahead.

What a powerful and awesome experience!! Just the fact that God loves me enough to give me a heads up on something that seemed like "no big deal" tells me that those "no big deal" things can turn into "BIG DEAL" things!! God has the end of the road vision.

We can only see a few steps in front of us, if that, and have no idea how things will play out, but God is all knowing and can see the beginning and the end!!

Picture this: Missing out on that job over something seemingly "small," losing out on the promotion over something "tiny", missing out on that new home or losing a chance at a new car over something that was "no big deal" or having friendships or more intimate types of relationships crumble or for that matter not even materialize because of something that appeared to be "trivial"... YET, God's Grace and Mercy gives us opportunities to re-focus and to miss near hits.

I think about my son, and how it gives me so much joy when I'm able to give him something he wants regardless of if he asked me for it or not, and how much it bothers me when he does something that hinders me from being able to bless him at that moment. I try to guide him just so that I can give him something special once he gets it together. I want him to act right so that I can get the pleasure of seeing the look on his face when Mommy gives him a reward for doing what I expect of him. God is the same way; He so much wants to able to bless us, but many times as it is with my son, He can't bless us at the time that He wants to because we do little things that hinder Him from doing so, and like I do with my son, He gives us hints and warnings that allow us to get back on track. Once we've done that, then He blesses us and gets excited when sees how much we appreciate His gifts.

How grateful I am that God sent that little tip, letting me know that the thing I thought was nothing, no big deal, trivial, insignificant, corny, and straight out stupid, had the potential to trip me up and allow a blessing to be delayed or terminated all together. It's one thing to lose out on something because of a big thing, but how hurtful is it when we lose something or miss an opportunity because of something small, something that can't even compare to what could have obtained, over something that really was stupid!!

Chapter 25

Integrity

It would seem that God has me waking up early in the morning so He can teach me and develop me into the woman whom He has called me to be.

This morning I woke up thinking about integrity and being a woman of integrity is doing right when people don't know you're doing right. Do right because it's right, no matter who knows it.

God began to show me that what I do when people are not around determines if I am a woman of integrity or not. If married, do I entertain certain conversations, or get involved with various activities that will disrespect my spouse just because they aren't with me and will never know? Integrity says that I will be faithful and respectful when together or when I'm away from him.

Integrity will take a firm stand when nobody is around to witness an offense, and no one is there to give you props for doing the right thing. Someone with true integrity doesn't need a reward for doing the right thing; he/she does the right things simply because it's the right thing.

Spiritual integrity says that no matter what, I represent God in all my actions, and if nobody ever acknowledges it, what God expects of me is what I will always stand for, because true integrity is always in operation. Integrity will consistently ask, *'Can God trust you? Can those whom God has placed in your life trust you? Can you be trusted in public, AND in secret?*

My desire is to be a woman of integrity, someone who will do right even if the only one who knows I did the right thing is me. To be a woman to whom God can say yes, I can trust Andrea, and whose reputation among those I have relationships with is one of trust and spiritual integrity. Am I there yet? No, I continue to strive, but my heart's desire is to be identified by God.

It can be so easy to get off-track and find yourself doing things because you know nobody is around to see what you're up to, but harder when you know that the only person who will know your choice is you. It's at those times when you are tested that will prove if you are walking in integrity, or if that is an area of your life where you need to do more work.

Chapter 26

Transformed

A TRANSPARENT MOMENT.... but a moment with a purpose. I have dated and have been married in the past, but to date I have never been taken on a date, treated to dinner, had my birthday celebrated by the person in my life, had a Valentine's Day, had a Christmas, or experienced those nice things that gentlemen do when they're in relationships. I have gone all out, spent money, did things "just because" but I don't know what that means in the reverse. Now by NO MEANS do I blame that on my ex-spouse or on past relationships, the blame stops with myself. Why, you ask? Because back then I didn't know something that I ABSOLUTELY know now; I know my worth, and I know my value!!

I know that while I may not be perfect, I am worth being given the things that I give out. I don't specifically mean "things," but it is in their attitude. I am worth the same giving spirit in someone as what I have and give.

Sometimes we get so beat down by hurt that we don't fully grasp whom we are; we don't see ourselves as the jewels we are. When you have a precious piece of jewelry, you don't treat it like you would costume jewelry; you treat it differently because its value is higher. So NOW I treat myself as the "sapphire" (I like sapphires) I am rather than just a blue painted rock!! I hear the statement often that you can't expect someone to treat you with value if you don't treat yourself as something of value. This is such a true statement! I was NEVER a person who passed myself around, but I WAS a person who accepted any old thing. (Notice I said WAS).

If I wasn't treated like I wanted, I hung in there thinking things would change if I continued being the sweet woman I was. However, how many know that sometimes you have to demand change and not just look for it to happen!! God did a transformation in me so that while waiting is hard, I can't allow myself to be on the "marked down/clearance rack" by settling for less than not only what I deserve, but what I am willing to give.

I believe in giving nothing less than 100% in relationships, friends and otherwise. Anything less than my best does not sit right with me. I have turned down requests because I didn't feel I could give my best. So, if I am committed to giving someone my best and treating someone as the priceless gem they are, then why accept less for myself? I am soooooo very thankful for the transformation that God did in my life, and for allowing me to see myself as He sees me.

Chapter 27

Giving Good Gifts

I love how God uses everyday things to teach me a lesson or point out important aspects of His character. I know all parents get that wonderful feeling when they can get something outside of the basic needs for their children, when they can buy something a child has asked for, or they know their child would like. When you see your child working hard, and then getting them the things they'd like gives a special feeling!! This is an especially good feeling for single parents who financially have all the responsibility on them.

Sometimes you can't do as much as you'd like for your child. Sometimes you have to tell them no, or not this time, but they deserve some of the extras. My heart is glad this evening because I was able to bless my son with an early Christmas gift! He was so excited and showed so much appreciation!! My son of course isn't perfect, and now that he is getting older and he is growing into a nice young man, I was excited to be able to bless him. I could have waited until Christmas, but if the truth were told, Mommy was excited too!! Lol!

As I'm sharing, the scripture has come to mind that in short talks about how if we as parents get joy out of blessing our children, how much more joy does God get in blessing us with good gifts, His children who strive to please Him! (Matthew 7:11) It's awesome how that scripture just took on life!! My son strives to please me, even in his mistakes. In the same way I am striving to please God, even in my errors. As my son is learning and growing, he is experiencing the growing pains of life. Likewise, I am experiencing spiritual growing pains as I strive to be a woman of whom God can be proud!

Chapter 28

Free From Spiritual Chitterlings

Today I was laughing at a post where a friend of mine was talking about her detest for chitterlings when God used her grossed-out state to minister to me!

When I was a young girl, my family would often spend the holidays at the home of the late Bishop Marion and Bertha Shaw. The Shaw's loved and lived to entertain. Their house was ALWAYS filled with family, friends and church members. Cakes, pies, turkey, fried chicken, macaroni & cheese, potato salad and collard greens were "everyday" meals at the Shaw home! The house always had an aroma that would cause your stomach to rise up and take notice!! One year upon walking into the Shaw home, there was an aroma that was unfamiliar to me, a scent that was needless to say, very hard on the nose: CHITTERLINGS!! Up to that point I had heard of this "Soul Food" delight, but had never seen them, tasted them, and apparently had never tasted them.

As I walked into the kitchen to greet everyone, Bishop Shaw was at the sink with sleeves rolled up and was washing something that to me looked very slimy! I sat at the kitchen table watching him wash these long strands of "slime" trying to figure out what in the world they were. As much time as I spent growing up in the Shaw home,

Bishop Shaw still scared me a bit. He was a big man, and someone who didn't take any junk. But on this day my curious nature got the best of me so I opted to go over to the sink and investigate exactly what Bishop Shaw was doing. As I watched him drain the sink of water, refill it, adding salt and a little vinegar, washing each strand carefully just to let the water out again to repeat the process several times over, finally I just had the ask, "What is that?" It was then I learned the history of chitterlings, how they were the undesirable, castaway portions of the pig given to slaves to feed their families.

I learned how slave women turned trash into a means to feed their children! I watched as he continued to prepare them, seasoned them up, and cooked them, finally after this long process was over, I was given a bowl and a bottle of hot sauce and invited to try them. That day, 30+ years ago, was the first and the LAST time I ate chitterlings. I determined that while my dad's family was from the south, this northern born girl did not inherit the love of chitterlings! As we fast-forward through years of slave oppression, we as African Americans are free to go toschool, vote, own homes and cars, but yet we still cling onto chitterlings, an aspect of our past that we no longer are forced to eat out of survival but now we eat simply because that's what was passed down to us!

How many of us are holding on to spiritual chitterlings, aspects of our past that held us slaves? How many of us are now comfortable in mess, accept castaways, and ingest what is foul? How many of us don't know how to let go of those things that caused us so much pain so that we can walk in and enjoy the freedom Christ has offered us? How many of us struggle with the filth and slime given to us by that slave- owner Satan? There is a saying that declares that we shouldn't forget the past lest we repeat it, and while I am not writing this chapter as a protest against the eating of chitterlings, it is time to break away from the trash and filth given to us by the slave-master and embrace our freedom in Christ! It's time to leave the spiritual chitterlings alone and ingest the meat at the King's table!

Christ came that we may be free from bondage, free from the residue of sin, free from the backlash of hurt and abuse and embrace the freedom of God! We are no longer prodigal sons and daughters, who are forced to eat from the trough of the swine; but we can partake in the feast that Christ has prepared for us, the banquet He has prepared in our honor!! It's time to walk away from the nastiness of spiritual chitterlings, and allow ourselves to enjoy those things that Christ has for us, the ones whom He calls His own. We have been delivered from the hands of the slave master. Jesus specifically stepped into Hell to retrieve the ownership papers from the hands of Satan, so now we are His. We now walk in an abundant life, like sons and daughters of The King! God has and gives the best gifts to His children - not trash, not castaway items, not leftovers, or as unwanted items. Instead, He has offered us His best if we would simply forget those things, which are behind us, and reach toward those things, which are ahead!!

Chapter 29

 # NEW

Something old, something new. Out with the bad, in with the good. Old year, new year. We must discard the old before we can receive the new! When a woman moves into a new home, while she may take things from her former residence, she instinctively wants to get rid of the old things and replace them with new things. When a child gets ready to return to school after the summer vacation, they don't usually enter a new grade in the clothes from the year before; instead, they get new outfits. Often in our lives we need to let the old things go and reach towards the new. Sometimes while there may be nothing wrong with the old, we often get too comfortable with the old.

Have you ever owned a old piece of clothing, maybe a sweater or a worn-out pair of jeans? Those items could be 100 years old, but we keep them because we feel secure in them. They are soft and comfortable. Sometimes while there is nothing wrong with the old, God wants to stretch us, challenge us, increase us, develop us, and for that to happen, we have to get rid of that spiritual old security blanket and be open to the new things that God wants to bring into our lives. Those relationships that aren't helping us to strive for better may not be able to move forward with us. That ministry where we have been faithful may not be allowing us to grow.

That area where we have become lazy may be the same area where we may need a jump-start. God is always about increase, elevation and promotion, but sometimes in order to experience newness in God, we need to let go of some of the old things that have become weights in our lives.

New isn't always easy to embrace; those new sheets aren't always nice and soft at first, but as we continue to lie on them, they begin to tailor themselves to our bodies. God wants us to trust Him and let go of the old and embrace the newness of Him, and the freshness of His presence in our lives! Old things are passed away, and behold all things are become new! Let's not be afraid to let go of the old; instead, trust God that the new is far better than the past. In God, the "IS" is always better then what "WAS."

Chapter 30

SHOCKED and AMAZED

A friend of mine, Mark Anthony McCray, stated this quote: "Some people are going to be shocked to learn that God wasn't nearly as shocked, offended and upset about some peoples' behaviors as they were."

If you look at the word of God, nothing that people did ever shocked God. Nothing that anyone did ever caused Jesus' jaw to drop; not Saul's employment of the services of a witch, not David's assassination plot, not Moses' temper. And not the woman whom Jesus met at the well - nor the woman who was about to be stoned for being caught in an adulterous relationship; He was not surprised by any of it. Jesus wasn't surprised by Peter who denied him, nor by Thomas who doubted Him, nor Judas who betrayed Him.

Nothing ever caught God/Jesus off-guard or ruffled His feathers. Now, one could argue that because Jesus was God and man, He already knew what people would do, but I believe that His reasoning was more than that. Jesus knew that His purpose for coming was to die for all these mistakes, and that the purpose of him shedding His blood was to cover the errors, so in knowing that, why be shocked? Why be bent out of shape? God knew His purpose was about these people, and Jesus accepted and embraced the weaknesses of man. He accepted it, so nothing that people did caused Him to be disillusioned.

Often when we hear about the indiscretions and mistakes of people, we find ourselves in a state of shock and amazement. When a leader is accused of a crime, when someone was in an affair, or when someone does something that is clearly on the top ten list of "thou shalt nots" we take on a spirit of arrogance, as if we have NEVER engaged in various behaviors! PLEASE!! The difference between others and us is that WE simply DIDN'T GET CAUGHT!

Our business wasn't in the news, on the street, or on the tongues of the saints! God isn't shocked by our behavior because He knows that He has made provision for us to be forgiven and cleansed from all the mess in which we've fallen! How dare we take the "better than thou" stance by being "utterly shocked and amazed" by what people do? The word warns us to judge not lest we be judged. (Matthew 7:1-3) In other words, don't get all holy lest some of your less than stellar moments leak out to the public and your secrets be made known! The mercy of God doesn't allow for attitudes of shock or arrogance because His grace is renewed every morning. Every day that we get up and fill our lungs with air is another opportunity to get it right! Even if we wanted to shock God, it would be impossible; His Son's blood covered a multitude of sins, so the sins that we haven't thought of yet are already covered.

The sins we never thought we'd do are already covered, and the sins we'll never bring ourselves to do, or we didn't even know they existed are already covered! We can't shock God! And, if you're like me, as I look at some of the things I've done, some of the things I thought about doing, and some of the things I attempted to do but failed, I'm GLAD it is impossible to shock and amaze God. Whew!!

Chapter 31

If Wolves Looked Like Jamie Foxx

People who are close to me know that secretly I am in love with Jamie Foxx! I was never a fan of "In Living Color", but when he came out with his own show and I heard him sing. I was slain!! Lol! He's sexy as all get out (but I digress) (lol). In any fairytale I have read, the villain in the story is very easily recognized by the reader but goes unnoticed by the character.

Snow White didn't recognize that "old woman" who was offering apples was actually the witch. Little Red Riding Hood sensed, or discerned something, but didn't recognize the wolf at Grandma's immediately. Even Simba, who was around his Uncle Scar often in the Lion King, didn't see that his beloved uncle was a sneak and later didn't realize that he was also a murderer.

Satan doesn't always dress the wolves and foxes in our lives in recognizable attire. Often, they come wrapped in sexuality, wrapped in a deep voice, wrapped in a banging body, wrapped in a clergy collar or choir robe. Little Red Riding Hood sensed something was wrong with Grandma. She observed a difference in her eyes, ears and teeth, and she heard a difference in the vocal tone. Now if the wolf was dressed like Jamie Foxx, the story might not have ended in victory! This is the devil's strategy, to camouflage reality with deception, while making things look like truth!

How many of us have seen a fruit basket or a plant only to realize that the fruit is plastic and the plant is fake? DECEPTION! or how many of us got ourselves connected to Mr. or Mrs. "Right" just to find out they were far from right, but very wrong? DECEPTION!!

Fool's gold, counterfeit money, and manmade gems all look good, but it's a deception, an attempt to trick the senses into thinking that something fake is real. It's a mirage, a lie!! Discernment must be a part of our daily walk; it must always be activated. Without discernment, we are subject to being lead in directions that may look good but won't be good. We may end up falling into traps where we can't climb out.

Eve saw a piece of fruit that looked good, and I'm sure it even tasted good, but everything that looks good isn't always good, as she later found out. Discernment, that spiritual radar, is what keeps us in alignment with God. The "Jamie Foxes'" of the world can't overwhelm us; we must keep our focus, maintain spiritual awareness, and not allow our human senses to cloud us. We must maintain a posture of spiritual tunnel vision, keeping our eyes focused only on Christ.

Chapter 32

Carpe Diem!!

2 Corinthians 5:17
"Therefore if any man be in Christ, he is a new creature: old things are passed away; behold, all things are become new."

As we look at the last Sunday in this year, as we begin counting down the final hours of an old year that is about to pass away and in just a short time we will walk into the newness of a fresh new year. One awesome thing about God is that every day that we wake up and fill our lungs with air is an opportunity to make right what went wrong the day before. It's a chance to repent, pick ourselves up, dry our tears, get back in the saddle and try again! God doesn't hold what happened yesterday against us. He stands by, cheering us on our new day and making Himself available should we call.

God's greatest delight is to see us succeed. Perhaps the past 12 months weren't your most stellar year, and perhaps you saw yourself doing and saying things did not represent God's best in you. Perhaps you failed that divine exam and then failed the make-up exam. Perhaps God told you to go here and do this, but you opted to go there and do that. Maybe you didn't spend as much time with Him as you should have done, and you didn't show your gratitude as you should have, or you didn't worship like you should have done. Perhaps you were so caught up with your own issues that you forgot about Him. At some point we ALL fell short, we all let God down, we all didn't hit every mark, BUT the good news is that old things are getting ready to pass away!

Should God in His mercy allow us to walk into a new year, then everything that took place in this year will fall into God's sea of forgetfulness and we can walk in with a fresh clean slate! BUT, as much as God is gracious, as much as He is merciful, as much as He is slow to anger, let us not take Him or the time being given to us for granted. Just because it will be January 1st with 365 days ahead of us, let's not drag our feet and waste time so that this time next year we find that we have again not progressed in God, but instead we wasted all year just trying to get started again!!

It's not the time to stroll through the meadows of another year! It's time to thrust ourselves forward and attack those things that God has directed each of us to do. If nothing else, recent events in our country have proven that tomorrow is not promised, and that each day is precious, and at any time life could be snatched away! Often, we hear the phrase *Carpe Diem*, SEIZE THE DAY. It's time to seize the day, the time, the year that God has allotted us, to take His mandates and run with them, to make a priority out of every moment that God blesses us to have!!

Soon this year will be nothing but a memory; it would have passed away, buried, and never to be resurrected! HOWEVER, all things ahead of us are and will be new! We can't change what took place over the last 365 days, but with God's hand, we can change what happens in the coming 52 weeks. As good as God has been, we dare not waste the time He's gifting to us. Let the old habits, attitudes, behaviors, spirits stay buried in the past, and let's walk into the New Year renewed, ready and eager to do what God has called us to do! It's a decision that we all must make.

It's a choice that all who walked into our current year will not be able to make in this coming year. Will we drag the dead weight of the past year into your new year? Or will you celebrate all the new things that God wants to crown you with? At the end of the day, the choice is ours, and God will not force us to let go of our past and embrace the freshness of His Spirit. He won't beg us to forgive ourselves for our shortcomings and exchange our guilt for freedom. Those are things we have done and embrace ourselves.

If God's desires to bless us with life more abundantly, why then do we hang on to the chains that kept us bound in the previous year? So again, I say: "Therefore if any man be in Christ, he is a new creature. Old things are passed away; behold, all things are become new" (2 Corinthians 5:17). Let's forget the old and accept the new!!

Chapter 33

An Outer Body Experience

Have you ever heard someone relay an account of an accident where they describe having an outer body experience? This is where they're hovering over themselves watching as doctors and medical personal work to restore life back to them. Many describe this experience as life changing, they knew they were dead, but for whatever reason it was not their time and they are sent back to occupy their bodies and to move forward in the task designed for them.

Today I experienced a supernatural outer body experience! I decided to visit a friend, and while visiting, while nothing major or sinful had taken place (yet) there was potential (just keeping it real). As we watched a movie, God began to put an unsettled feeling in me, and started asking me questions, such as, *"Andrea why are you here? You know you really don't want to be here; you don't even like this person!"* Next thing I knew, I saw me hovering, while looking down at myself. Again, nothing remotely had taken place; the only thing I was doing was watching a movie, BUT God knew what was pending. It was nothing that I wanted, or nothing I went searching for, but it was something that could have been to my detriment!

When we ask God to keep us, shield us, protect us, guard us, and do so sincerely, God will use what seems like unconventional methods to get our attention. For me, it was an outer body experience. So how did my story end? As I hovered over myself, feeling more and more irritated with myself, KNOWING this was NOT what I desired, I heard myself say aloud, "Andrea what are you doing!?!" The friend at this point had dozed off. I got my shoes, my purse, tapped him and said I had to go, and that was that!! I was done!! I was saved to fight another day, and free from the bondage of condemnation.

God will keep us if we desire to be kept; the word clearly states that He will MAKE A WAY of escape!! I'm grateful today because I know He is preserving me for something I can't begin to imagine!! He wants me to thrive, achieve, and to be victorious!! As I drove down the highway, my heart rejoiced. There is nothing like knowing you won a battle and passed a test! While I'm sure more tests will come, I'm not going to dwell on the "next time" right now. All I know is that TODAY, at this moment, over this situation I am victorious!

Chapter 34

Healthy Living From the Inside Out

Often the things we do to maintain our physical bodies are the same things we need to do to maintain our spiritual health. In the same way that we focus on eating right/healthy, we should also focus on eating the right spiritual food, going to a 5-star spiritual restaurant (church), eating healthy snacks (reading the Word). As we make the effort to shower and keep our bodies clean physically, we must maintain a clean spiritual lifestyle by staying away from things that will make us spiritually dirty, such as gossip, back biting, and judging.

Just like we exercise to get rid of excess weight, we must cut off those things that weigh our spirits down by cutting off people who bring us down. We must practice spiritual habits that will build us up, such as reading the Word, and engaging in praise and worship and personal devotions. Principles and practices to maintain the physical body will also work for our spiritual stability. God is a holistic God, and wants us to be healthy and whole in our minds bodies and spirits. We just need to apply ourselves so we can be the healthy servants that He needs us to be.

Chapter 35

Who Will Step Up and Help Carry the Cross?

One Saturday evening I was watching the Turner Classic Movie epic, "The Robe," where there was a scene of Jesus stumbling as He was carrying the cross to Calvary, and Simon stepped in to carry the cross for him. As I was watching, this question dropped into my spirit: "Who will step up to help carry the cross?" Who will take the burdens of people on their shoulders? Who will help carry the weight of hurt and suffering that people are experiencing, on their shoulders? Who will carry someone's tears? Who will grab someone's hand and help pull him or her to their victory?

Jesus carried the burden of the world on His shoulders, but it is our responsibility as His ambassadors to carry and bear the burdens of others. We get so wrapped up in our own issues and situations that often we forget those who are struggling next to us too. There are people who are fighting and clawing trying to make it to the top of their Golgotha in the same way that we are. The word of God tells us to bear the infirmities of the weak. We must do better at helping our brothers and sisters make it. How can we celebrate our victories knowing that those around us are striving to make it? It shouldn't be so easy to celebrate when someone else is crying. It's time to reach back and grab the hand of those climbing up the same mountain behind us and ensure that they can rejoice as we rejoice. It is an honor to serve, and an honor to be commissioned by God to help Him carry the burdens of others. We ought to carry the cross of others joyfully knowing that at some point we will be in a position where we will need an agent of God to assist us in our journey to the top of our mountain.

Chapter 36

Follow the Yellow Brick Road

I have a question. What if the road Dorothy followed wasn't color-coded and she wasn't wearing heels that clicked? Would she have walked by faith and not by sight?

"Now faith is the substance of things hoped for, the evidence of things not seen." Hebrews 11:1 (KJV). Faith is when we trust God blindly, where we see situations, but we don't see the solution. Often, when we trust God, He doesn't give us the road map; we don't have a yellow brick road to follow. No matter who is around or how accomplished they are in thought and theory, only God has the answer; He is the only one who has the solution. Faith says that you trust God enough to allow Him to work things out in the way that He sees fit.

You trust His ability and His expertise. Faith says that I have no clue how I'm going to get out of this situation, but I trust that God will provide the way of escape. Like Abraham, God will provide the ram. "Faith to reach the unreachable, Faith to fight the unbeatable, Faith to remove the unmovable, and Faith that stands the invincible."

Chapter 37

Life Is the Dash

Some years ago there was a BET reality show featuring Damon Dash called *"The Ultimate Hustler"* similar to *The Apprentice*, people were given assignments to grow or increase business within the Hip-Hop arena. Mr. Dash, who has a strong work ethic, always ended the show with this phrase, "LIFE IS THE DASH."

"LIFE IS THE DASH." I have heard this preached at a few Homegoing services, but until we get a firm handle on how short and fragile life is, we can't embrace and understand the depth of this statement. If you look at any headstone, you will see a birth date and a death date, but separating these two dates is the dash symbol, a short little line that represents life. Every day that we are blessed to arise from sleep, we are walking and living in that dash, in a moment of time that we will never have again. So, the question to ask ourselves is: How are we spending our time? What are we doing with that dash of time we are allotted? If we are honest, many of us have to admit that so much time has been wasted on foolishness. We've wasted time with the wrong people, and wasted it doing unproductive things; and wasted in wrong relationships. Time has been wasted due to dragging our feet and not making the most of every opportunity given and wasting time we can't retrieve or repeat. I think about my time in college, my first time away from home. Young, a little daring, that first year was crazy! I failed a few of my classes, and I hooked up someone that was hooked up with a few others.

We were always skipping curfew, and not showing up for class. I was a 16/17-year-old freshman who was enjoying her first taste of real freedom and it was delicious! But the moment of change came when the dean of women called me into her office one morning after getting caught the night before sneaking into the dorm waaaaaaaay past curfew to let me know that if I didn't get my hind parts together, I was not going to be able to return the following year! Now that may have been just a scare tactic because in the big picture I wasn't doing anything REALLY out there, but I did know that because I started Atlantic Union College at age 16 that she actually did care and was looking out for me.

It was enough for me to be reminded that if I got kicked out of school, there was potential for my parents to kill me so I quickly took hold of my reigns and got myself together! (I want to have fun, but I wasn't crazy!!) I took those failed classes over during the summer and from that point (at least academically) I had a successful college experience. I had wasted a year, but I was able to regroup, put my priorities in perspective and do what I needed to do with the time given. But that is not always the case. I was blessed, but it's not all the time that we are given a second chance. Sometimes we have to live with our mistakes, if we live at all! I think about friends I lost in high school due to drinking and driving after the prom.

There was no second chance, no repeat, and no do over; their dash line was cut abruptly. We all, at one time or another, have wasted time that Christ has given us. In our youth we feel that we have plenty of time to live for Christ, but more than ever the lives of youth are being cut short. We tell ourselves we are strong and healthy and think that we can dedicate our lives to God later, but disease attacks the body at any age! Bottom line, we don't know when our dash line will end. We don't know when our today will be our last, so what are we doing with our dash, with our time? Are we sharing the awesomeness of Christ with others? Are we living examples? Do we take time to bless and encourage others? Do we simply let them know that they are important to God? Do we love on our children? Do we show our spouses how much they bless our lives? Are the words coming out of our mouths speaking life into someone else? Is our time spent serving those whom God has placed in our sphere? Or are we about gossip, hating on each other, tearing each other down, or being ambassadors of Satan instead of Christ? When the dash has ended, and that final date is recorded and the preacher is speaking about the life we lived, will he be able to truly share what we did to represent God, or will he have to embellish the facts a bit? This is something to think about....

We are allotted a certain amount of time, and when our dash is turned over to God to evaluate and judge, what will God say about our dash moment? Will He say, "Well done" or "Depart from me?" My former pastor's wife Sis. Mary Seemore use to sing a song often: "Remember only what you do for Christ will last, remember only what you do for Christ will last, only what you do for Him, will be counted in the end, only what you do for Christ will last."

"LIFE IS THE DASH." What will you be able to submit to God once your dash line has ended? Think about the length of a dash; it's a short mark, just a quick twist of the wrist. Life isn't long, we are given a quick twist of God's hand, and with such a short period of time, can we really afford to waste even a single second?

Chapter 38

As Soon As I Stop...

Sometimes we need to really take apart words to songs to grasp the REAL meaning, what the writer is REALLY trying to covey. I was having a moment taking apart the words to this song and making it personal:

"AS SOON (the second I decide to release myself from the situation) AS I (Andrea) STOP WORRYING - WORRYING (about) HOW THE STORY (is going to end) ENDS, IF I (Andrea) LET GO (let go of all the overthinking, how can I do this, what's going to happen, how can I make it happen, what if I don't have it when I need it, how will I take care of my son, etc.) AND I (Andrea) LET GOD, LET GOD HAVE HIS WAY (let God do His job and let Andrea do Andrea's job) THAT'S (that is) WHEN THINGS START HAPPENIN' (when I allow God to do His job and I take my hands out the pot, that's when things begin to change) WHEN I STOP LOOKING AT BACK THEN, (when i stop looking at what things look like to my naked eye) WHEN I (Andrea) LET GO AND I (Andrea) LET (allow) GOD, LET (choose to allow God to do His thing) GOD HAVE HIS WAY!" (DeWayne Woods, Album: Introducing DeWayne Woods & When Singers Meet, 2006)

Chapter 39

FREE AT LAST

Looking at the epic 'NORTH and SOUTH', the North had won the war and the former slaves have begun leaving the homes of their previous slave-owners. The interesting part is that some ex-slaves left the plantations, and some ex-slaves stayed. Those who left had no place to go and had no way of supporting themselves and their families, but they left with the faith that they would make it! They may not know how, but they knew they would overcome any obstacle.

Now the ex-slaves who opted to stay were physically no different than the ones who left except for one thing: they lacked hope, they lacked faith, they lacked freedom of mind! Those that left said to themselves, "We have nothing, but we will not stay in the place that represents captivity. We will walk in freedom!" Many of us have been set free from a variety of things: bad relationships, depression, addictions, toxic relationships, and so on. However, once delivered we often we lose our deliverance because we fail to remove ourselves from the place of our captivity and become re-infected. Or we believe that we are strong and return to the slave quarters, which cause us to slip back into the same thing from which God delivered us. Much like the flu, if we place ourselves in harm's way of illness, we risk getting sick or being re-infected with sickness.

Why? Because our spiritual immune system isn't strong enough to handle those things from which God delivered us. Being free means walking away from the things that held us captive.

That means not looking back for that last glance; it means breaking free from the grave clothes and walking in liberty! As an ex-slave to our past, we can't stay connected to the plantation, the slave quarters, and the Massa that ruled over us! We must come out from among them and embrace freedom! Don't credit yourself for strength; you don't have it yet. If you know you are still weak to his sweet nothings, then don't think you can "just hang out." If you can't have "just a sip," then don't offer a toast. If her perfume makes you weak, don't think it will be easy to "just" cuddle up! Flee from the slave Master's hold; don't continue to stay on his land. If Christ has blessed you with freedom, you may not know where to go or what to do next, but you must leave the place of your slavery and trust God to lead you to "The North," to your Promised Land.

Chapter 40

What Kind of Praise Does YOUR God Deserve?

One of the Associate Pastors at my church inspired this piece. It has given me food for thought. This question, if answered honestly, may change how you praise the God you serve.

Have you ever asked yourself what kind of "god" you serve? The kind of "god" you serve will dictate the kind of praise you give him. If you serve a "sometimes" god he naturally deserves just a sometimes praise. If you serve an "average" god, then it is only fitting that you give him an average praise! HOWEVER, "if" you serve an "incredible" God, you owe Him no less than an incredible praise! Why? Because as the song ministered by Youthful Praise Choir states, "An INCREDIBLE God DESERVES an INCREDIBLE praise!"

Ask yourself this question: has God done anything incredible in your life? Did He do something that neither you, nor anyone else, could not have accomplished on your own? Has God proven Himself to be incredible to you? Now once you have answered in the affirmative, would you not agree that a God, as incredible as our God is, deserves nothing less than an incredible praise? Anything less would be disrespectful and a sign of un-appreciation for all

He is, all He's done and all He promises to do! An incredible God, such as the One we serve, deserves nothing less than an incredible praise!! MY God deserves an incredible praise. What does YOUR God deserve?

Chapter 41

He Saw the Best In Me

I was up early one morning thinking about how far I've come over the last few years. When you've experienced mental abuse, it becomes a pattern to see yourself not as how God sees you, but instead as how people see you. When situations happen and things you wanted in your life fail, or people reject you, it is easy to accept the realities of others instead of the realities of Christ. It is easy to accept the worst of what people see.

You're not this, you're not that, this reason, that excuse, this is not right, that is not right, and the list of negative statements continues. BUT I'm so grateful not only that God saw and sees the best in me, but that over the years He has allowed my spiritual vision to change so that I see the best in me! I see where I've been and how far I've come. I see the errors, but I also see the growth! I see the Andrea who cried because of rejection but who now rejoices because she sees the bullet that was missed! When everyone else around could only see the worst in me, He saw the best in me, and then He allowed ME to see the best in me. Looking through the eyes of God are honest; they don't gloss over areas of your life that you need to work on and grow in, but they do allow you to see your potential in God and what you are becoming. Rejection still hurts, and what you see in the mirror may not be the image you want to see. We all desire acknowledgement from those we hold dear, BUT it is an awesome and beautiful thing when God can alter your vision and allow you to see the beauty in yourself in whom He delights! GRATEFUL that what people see in me are not and will never be the total of what God sees in me. Man looks at and sees the Physical, but God looks at and sees my heart. And, those with spiritual eyes and discernment, and those whom God has designed to attach to your life, will see only the best.

Chapter 42

Refuse To Be Robbed!

Fear is one of the biggest robbers in life, for it robs you of "what could be." Don't allow fear to stop you from starting with something/someone. Don't let fear stop you from going through with something/someone, and don't allow fear to stop you from seeing something/someone to the end. Fear will rob you of potential blessing!! I refuse to allow fear to keep me from the "what could be's" in my life!! REFUSE!!

REMEMBER THIS!! Faith and Fear are not siblings; they're not related! Faith and Fear are polar opposites! Fear will keep you AWAY from the awesome blessings of God, while Faith will draw you CLOSER to what God wants to bless you with!! I say it again! I REFUSE to allow fear to keep me from the blessings that God has for ME!!

Flowers From The Master's Garden

Chapter 43

Our "Good" –vs.- God's "Good"

God will never lie to us, and when He takes the time to show us something, we can be assured that what He has allowed us to see accurate information. Now it becomes our choice what He allowed us to see. "A "good" thing isn't always a "God" thing" (Pastor Bobbie)

I have said so many times that God really wants us to succeed. But for us to succeed, we have to have a keen sense of discernment. We have to be aware of our spiritual senses so that we can recognize those things that may not be good for us.

Fried chicken is good, but it isn't good for us. We may love it, but all that grease is not good for our bodies. That "once in a lifetime opportunity" may be good money, good benefits, but it may not be God's choice for us. Maybe God wants to save us from high levels of stress and frustrations, and maybe we want to maintain our family life instead of always being at the job. MAYBE God wants to bless us with something even better! That good man that good woman may be good in our eyes, everything we dreamed about, but maybe he/she is not the God woman, God man that He wants for us. They may be in ministry, love God, and serve Him to the best of their ability, but perhaps the call on your life and the call on their life doesn't line up.

God sees what we don't see. Our vision is limited, while Christ sees from the beginning to the end, He sees the obstacles and the pitfalls. He sees what we need, and not just what we want. He sees what will take us into our destiny!! Our "good" isn't always God's "good," and our "good" will never be as good as God's "good!" God's good is His best!! So why settle for simply "good," when God desires us to have His best!!

Chapter 44

A Pot of Boiling Water

As a child is in his/her mother's womb, he/she is like a large cast iron pot of boiling water simmering on the stove. The water is hot, and there is absolutely no flavor. This pot of water could become anything: from a huge pot of Georgia Sweet Tea to a large pot of rich Boston Clam Chowder. What this "pot of water" will turn into will depend on what ingredients are added.

From the moment that child is delivered, he/she is confronted with various experiences, good and bad, that add "seasonings," "vegetables," "meat," "sugar," "lemon" etc. that add character, and personality, to that plain pot of water. Only God knows what that pot of water will turn into after it is completed, but every single thing we go through contributes to what Christ wants us to be, whether we become that hearty pot of beef stew or if we become a pot filled with collard greens. The thing about it, as the ingredients are added to our pots, the things we go through, are not only for our benefit but for the nourishment of those whom God places to eat from our tables. One person may not be able to digest the collards from my pot, but the tasty chicken noodle soup from my brother's pot may be easier to digest.

When I think back over some of the experiences I have had over the years, I never thought I would survive simmering on the stove for as long as I have, with the heat being turned up. But now that the pot has had time to cool down and all the ingredients have had time to get in there, I see how all that I went through wasn't just to help me mature, but to share and bless someone else.

While we must be mindful of what ingredients we add to our pots, and mindful of who is adding ingredients to our pots, we have to remember that God is working it out for the greater good, the bigger picture! Someone we come in contact with is starving for what's inside our pot. Their spiritual stomachs are grumbling; they're waiting for someone to offer them a hearty bowl of food to cure the pain of an empty stomach.

As we serve them what Christ has created in us, we add to the miracle of God's healing, delivering and saving hand. Although things can get hot, and it can takes years to recover from hurts, issues, and betrayals, God sees who will benefit from the pot of food He has prepared within us.

Since we opted to keep trying, and we opted to fight through the tears, contain ourselves through anger, and smile when our trust has been shot to pieces; there are special blessings in store for us. Our prayers are getting ready to become realities! All the ingredients prepared us for who we are and who we will face. This is all a part of God's divine plan for our lives.

In all the good, bad and ugly, God will get the glory. You may not see what your end product will be while you are cooking, but know that who God is "cooking" you to be is made up from a one-of-a-kind secret recipe and designed to feed those who have a hunger and a craving eat something that's divinely unique.

Chapter 45

I Choose You AGAIN

Every day we must choose God, and every day we must recommit to Him. We must recommit to serving, trusting and following Him. Following God is something that requires letting God know that on this day He has our permission to order our steps, to guide our attitudes, and to regulate our speech.

Remember that God doesn't force us to do anything; we choose to submit, to give, to serve, and to love Him. If God means to us as much as we claim, we must choose Him daily! With so many options, and so many gods, my love for God causes me, implores me, and beckons me to choose Him each day. Before we begin our day, the moment we open our eyes we must choose God. Father, You mean so much to me on this day; I choose You again!

Chapter 46

We Are One

Relationships of any kind are about unity, with two people coming together and sharing a thought and concept. It's a duet, a ride down life's highway on a tandem bike, a waltz, synchronized swimming, with everyone moving in concert from the common goal. Have you ever watched Double-Dutch, and how awesome is it when after some practice both parties go at it together, where they are jumping, ducking, tucking and rolling, doing splits, leaping over each other and doing all sort of tricks and acrobatics together in sync and in harmony? No one person is the star, and no one person is trying to hoard the spotlight. It's about joining skills together to create an awesome production.

So, as we work to maintain and establish relationships, when issues surface, the question we must ask is if ALL parties involved are TRYING to jump together and just haven't worked out all the kinks yet, or is one person trying to be a Double-Dutch expert and not trying to let the other partner get in. If it's a matter of more practice, then more time is the answer.

Don't give up; press to work through issues! Relationships are precious and deserve the attention needed to maintain them. Time and effort is needed to get all the moves on one accord. However, there are times when we must divorce ourselves from people, when instead of encouraging us they are tearing down, or when their interest is not about the "we" but about the "I." The old saying is true, there is no "I" in team, so if you are in a relationship that is toxic, self- serving or unbalanced then it is time to remove yourself from the Double-Dutch team and find a tandem bike and a person who desires to pedal through life WITH you!!

Chapter 47

The Three Little Pigs

The children's story of "The Three Little Pigs" is an interesting story. Three pigs were sent off to build their own homes. If the parents of these pigs did their job effectively, then each pig was given the tools and the know-how on how to build a proper home that would withstand the elements. However, each pig went out and selected different materials on which to build their houses, and as the story goes, two of the pigs didn't build sturdy homes, so that when the wolf came he was able to blow the homes down. The home of the third pig withstood the wolf's attempts to destroy it.

In this story, the lesson I have learned is that we need to be concerned with the materials we are using to build our spiritual homes. I am so glad that I am able to see ME, MY HOUSE, the place where I reside in God. I can see the areas of my life where screws need to be tightened, and nails need to be hammered back down; or where areas of my house simply need to be replaced! So often we look at "other homes" and judge the condition of the homes. We notice that shingles are hanging, and the front doors could use some fresh paint; the grass needs to be cut, or that deck is missing some planks. Yet, we fail to look at the condition of their own homes and yards and make the proper repairs. When storms come, normally they don't attack "the block" but they will affect individual homes. Have you ever walked through a neighborhood that has experienced a tornado or hurricane, and out of ten homes, eight may be demolished, but two are standing untouched? We cannot be concerned if someone else's house doesn't look up to par, we have to ensure that the house we live in is strong, sturdy, and able to withstand the elements of life. Our job is to tend to our own house and yard. God is the Master Landlord and is perfectly capable of managing the other "properties" on our block.

Chapter 48

No Trespassing

We do not have to allow just anyone to get close to us. Who we allow in our lives is a deliberate choice. I have to choose to let you come through the gate of my life, and even then I have the choice on how far on my property I will let you come. Experience teaches you not to allow everyone to run up on your property. Everyone will not treat your life with the same care as you treat it so it becomes your responsibility to yourself to protect your yard. When I was a kid, the front lawn was my dad's pride and joy! We were allowed to play in the backyard, but the front yard was off-limits.

When friends came to play, it was my sister's and my responsibility to let them know where we could play, and if someone opted not to listen and venture on my dad's nice green grass, or in my mom's flower bed then they weren't allowed to play in our yard. My dad would say just because others don't take care of their yard doesn't mean that they could come and trample on ours. If people won't respect, honor, cover, pray, and treat your yard, i.e. your life as God has designed for it to be treated, then you have the right to keep them at bay. You don't have to invite them into your inner circle.

Jesus had twelve friends, but out of the twelve, three were closer to Him than the rest. And, although Judas was able to get close enough to Him to betray Him, it was still Jesus' choice to allow him to get that close. Jesus knew that Judas was part of completing His mission. If Jesus didn't want Judas close to Him, then one word out of His mouth would have taken Judas down quickly!

Be mindful of who you allow in your yard and choose wisely. The people whom you allow to come through the gate of your life should add to the beauty of your yard and should not bring the value of your property down!

Chapter 49

Care Instructions

Most items that we buy come with care instructions. The label on the inside of a clothing item will tell us how to wash it, and an electronics manual will tell us how to treat the item so that it runs at peak performance. Jewelry comes with instructions for its care and cleaning. Every item has its own set of care instructions that are tailored to that specific item. You don't care for silk the same way you care for cotton, and you don't care for your laptop in the same way that you care for your iPad. Every item is specific in its care and maintenance.

When God gives you something, or shows you something, what He's about to give you will show and equip you with the know-how on how to take care of it, how to maintain it, and how to keep it. You will be given specialized instructions! Every situation isn't the same, and every person has different care instructions. If you desire to keep what God has given you, or maintain what He's is about to give you, then take the time to read, study and implement the instructions! You can't walk into a new relationship or marriage with the same set of instructions from the last one. You can't walk into that new position just like you walked out of the last one. You can't maintain your new ministry at the same level at which you maintained the last ministry! With anything new comes greater responsibility, and one cannot maintain the new with the old instructions.

As I look at the new thing coming into my life, I am excited as I'm "viewing" the instructions and listening as God is directing me on how to handle this new thing!! "Handle With Care," "Pray Without Ceasing," "Talk With Respect," and "Massage The Heart With Loving Words." Follow the instructions to keep what you have, and to maintain what is coming.

READ AND IMPLEMENT THE INSTRUCTIONS!

Chapter 50

 ## Fear -vs- Faith

Fear is a powerful emotion, based on past painful experiences that will keep you from your future. Fear is a protective mechanism the mind uses to shield us from potential pain. Fear is the only emotion that can literally paralyze and will have you refusing to move forward! Fear is the polar opposite of faith; you can trust God and live in fear to the point where you are stuck in your past and present! Faith propels you forward, while fear will keep you glued to one spot!!

Fear will keep you from applying for that better position because you were denied previously. Fear will keep you from getting medical attention because you are afraid of what they'll find. Fear will keep you from trying to purchase a home because you're scared your credit will hinder you from obtaining a mortgage. Fear will keep you from becoming a husband or wife and being joined with someone who will adore you because your heart was hurt in a past relationship. Fear will keep you from the "life more abundantly" status that Christ has promised to His children.

A few weeks ago I visited the dentist to have some dental work done. It was the first time in a while that I had been there, and while I'm not one who is scared easily, this was something that had me gripped in fear. Traveling back some years, I was working for a school that didn't offer health insurance, so dental insurance was not available to me. Such out-of-pocket expenses can leave a huge hole in one's pocket. Well there came a time when I needed a tooth pulled, so it was suggested that I go to the state which had various dental labs designed for uninsured clients and the cost would be little.

Already in pain, I found an office close to me and went. When I was set up to have the tooth pulled, I was given a very TINY needle of Novocain and soon after the doctor began to pull the tooth. When I literally screamed in pain I was then notified with two assistants holding me that because I was uninsured that the tooth was coming out with that little bit of medication and with that he went back to pulling the tooth, which didn't come out easily. To say I have NEVER in my life felt that kind of pain before was an understatement! Even now, years later, the memory brings tears to my eyes!! That experience kept me FAR from the dentist for years, even after I started receiving insurance. I was blessed not to have major issues, but this year I made the choice to get over my fears and to start getting things in the best possible health and to set a good example for my son, which meant I needed to visit the dentist. My co-worker had been raving about a dentist so I decided to get it together and go. Upon walking into the office, my blood pressure must have been through the roof! My heart was racing, and my hands were sweating! I was AFRAID!! But the dentist was so kind and so gentle that what once WAS my biggest fear is now a place that I can go with ease, knowing that my dental needs will met.

The fear of our past, fear of hurt, fear of rejection, and fear of pain will keep us from the abundance of God! Fear is a weight, and God admonishes us to lay aside every weight that so easy besets us, and so easily can overtake us!! Faith says, God I may have been hurt, and this happened to me in the past. I don't know what the future holds, BUT I trust You. And even if pain does happen, I trust You to heal me and to take me through whatever may come! Faith tells God that I surrender myself to You!! There are people who won't step in elevators, who won't sit in small spaces, who won't eat certain things or go certain places because they are afraid. The past has marked them with doubt!! Trust in the Lord, have faith in the Lord with all your heart and lean not on your own understanding!! Let go of fear and allow God to lead you. When you trust The Leader, there IS no reason to doubt or fear because you have confidence in their abilities!! Today I encourage you to swap fear for faith and let God order your steps! God will not lead you to destruction, but into peace!! The word of God let us know to fear NOT, for He is with us!! Fear keeps us away from God, while faith will always draw us closer.

Chapter 51

Please Allow Me to Have This "OUT OF THE BOX" Moment

QUESTION: What if it turned out that there was no God? What if the way I choose to live my life was "a waste?" What if when I die this was it? Would the way I've tried to live my life all these years still be worth it? ANSWER: ABSOLUTELY! Let's look at why. Is not jumping from bed to bed, something good? YES! Is treating people with love and respect, something good? YES! Is walking in integrity, something good? YES! Is not having several children with several different fathers or not having children at all, something good? YES! Is treating my body with respect, not ingesting things that will hurt it or impair it, something good? YES! Is my belief in someone who only promoted a life of love, peace, joy, and righteousness, something good? YES!

Now, please make no mistake! I KNOW God and believe in all that the Bible says He is and know what He's proven to be in my life personally and thus serve Him as such. But, for those who doubt, why live a life of destruction, a life of hurt, an unfulfilled life, or a life that's always searching for more when you can put your trust, your confidence, and your faith in God, knowing that only what you do for HIM will stand now and forever.

Chapter 52

There'll Be Time Enough For Countin' When the Dealin's Done

It's interesting to me how certain songs will enter my mind at different times, sparking thoughts I know are specifically downloaded into my spirit by God. The chorus to this old Kenny Rogers classic *"The Gambler"* (Written by: Don Schilitz, Artist: Kenny Rogers, 1978) is such an example:

"You've got to know when to hold 'em Know when to fold 'em
Know when to walk away Know when to run
You never count your money When you're sittin' at the table
There'll be time enough for countin' When the dealin's done"

Timing is everything. We have to learn how to discern the time to be where God wants us to be, at the time that He wants us there. Often, we are either running ahead of God, or dragging behind Him. But if we learn to be in alignment with God's timing, we will be able to see the hand of God and His purpose more clearly. Running ahead of God can have us walking into things that aren't prepared for us, while lagging behind and dragging can cause us to miss divinely appointed opportunities. Even the good things that God has for us to do or to be a part of are subject to His perfect timing. King David had the desire to build a temple for the Lord, which would house the Ark of the Covenant, but God's desire was not that it be built during his reign, but during the reign of his son Solomon. TIMING!

Maybe that job, that ministry position is yours, but God's desire for you to walk in it is not now, but later. For now, He wants you to work and serve where you are. TIMING! Perhaps he is your husband, or she is your wife, but God is doing something in you both so that your marriage will be until death. TIMING! Maybe those friends want you to do things that God has called you out of, and God is telling you that it's time to separate yourself. TIMING!

Maybe God has told you that it's time to leave those comfortable surroundings and go where He is leading you. TIMING! In this season, I see how God has prepared me for what's to come. It hasn't always been easy to wait, since my time never seems to match God's time schedule. Some things take time to change and develop. In the same way that it takes time to gain weight, it takes time to lose it. Behaviors and habits were developed over the years, and they take time to shed. In the same way that it takes a cake some time to bake before it is officially a cake, I see how God has taken the time to develop me into a woman who is very different than who she was in the past.

> TO HAVE WHAT GOD WANTS YOU TO HAVE,
> YOU MUST BE WHERE GOD WANTS YOU TO BE AT
> THE SPECIFIC TIME THAT HE WANTS YOU THERE!

Chapter 53

Choosing To Let God Choose

As I think about choices, the decisions I make now don't always yield fruit on the spot, but a day, a week, a month, or a year later, the seeds of choice I sowed now begin to surface. I had an assistant pastor, who, when he would make the call to discipleship, would say: "No matter if you choose to spend eternity in Heaven or choose to spend eternity in Hell, be informed! If you choose not to make Christ the head of your life, be informed on the long-term effects of your choice."

That statement would often get a chuckle, but for me it always stirred something in my thinking process. Why, because every choice I make, from what I eat, to where I work, to who I'm friends with, to what I say, or who I allow into my life on an intimate level, will have direct and long- term effects on my life, as well as on the life of my son. Choosing to listen to my flesh instead of God comes with a heavy price tag. My choices must be the choices that God has ordained for me. If you look at the bad choices you have made throughout your life, many of us can testify that one choice, or one decision left a residue that took an extended amount of time to heal That one late night call or visitor, that one act in anger, that one curious try, that one curse, that one dare, came at a cost! Just one time driving drunk, texting behind the wheel, or sleeping with that person could lead to death! Sometimes you only get once chance to make the right choice!!

If we do nothing else, each day, before our feet touch the floor in the morning, we must make the choice to allow God to order our steps, and to order our choices. If we make that one choice every day, by making the choice to submit to the choices of God, we are allowing Him to speak to us and change our thinking that will help us make better choices for ourselves.

After so many wrong Andrea-dictated choices that ended badly, which took years for me to recover, I can't afford to yield to choices based on my limited vision. While I can only see as far as the next second that God allows me to live, He sees the effects of my choices 5, 10, 15, and 20+ years ahead. Allowing God to direct our choices allows us to bypass those things that we can't see, we aren't ready for and never will be prepared to handle. Allowing God to choose for us gives us, at the very least, the information that says God's choice is better. We may not know why, and we may not have all the details associated with God's choices for us, but what we do know is that God's way will always be better than ours, so in that respect, allowing God to choose for us, knowing that His way is best, is really all the information we need!!

Chapter 54

Our Stories

EVERYONE has stories, and each story, whether it's a novel or a short story, contributes to who they are, and why they do what they do, the way they do it. Unless we personally wrote a person's story, read a person's story, or were there every second the story was being written, we have no right to judge how they relate to various aspects of life, because we don't know what stories created them and caused them to be who and what they are! We don't know why that woman carries herself in that particular way, right or wrong.

We aren't sure why she craves attention, or what dictates her reactions. We don't know the stories that caused him to erect the walls that surround his heart, or what novel makes him freeze up when she tries to touch his heart and offer him love. We don't know, and because we don't know why she cries, why he is afraid, or why she wants love but runs when it comes, we don't have the right to judge behaviors. Instead, in love, let's offer our experiences, our understanding, and offer them the love and compassion of God that will allow them to write new stories. The new stories will realign their walk and how they respond to pages yet to be written.

Chapter 55

Word Of the Day: "SUSTAINER"

Have you ever heard the expression, "driving on fumes?" In literal terms, the person is saying is that their gas tank is pretty much on empty, and they are driving on a drop of gas. Sometimes we hear this term in reference to a person's ability to function, which usually means that they are exhausted and are operating on a tiny bit of strength.

God is our SUSTAINER, and when we are exhausted, God gives us what we need to sustain us one more day. In music, the word, "sustain" means to hold or extend a note. If you hit a note on a keyboard, the notes can continue to be heard once the key is released. God is so awesome that when we are down to nothing, at the end He will prolong our strength and endurance. He will extend our finances and stretch what's in our refrigerator. He can extend the gas in the car, and prevent the lights, gas, and water from being turned off. He does this out of His profound love for us! I am reminded of the woman who had only enough oil and flour for one more meal for herself and her son, but her obedience to the man of God and her faith in God caused a miracle. God took her last and extended it indefinitely!!

I am thanking God that He loves me enough to sustain me when I feel like I am at the end of my rope, and when I'm physically, emotionally and spiritually tired. When it seems like I'm down to nothing, God comes along and gives me just a little bit more to keep me. Sometimes it seems like God has let go of us and is allowing us to drown, but right before our heads go underwater, God reaches down and sustains our life.

"He is the Keeper (the Sustainer) of my soul..."

Chapter 56

He Says I Am Beautiful

Candice Glover, American Idol 2013 winner, enticed the ears of listeners with her single, "I Am Beautiful." If you were watching intently as Candice mesmerized the audience, you would have witnessed two very distinct gestures; one where she glanced upward, and then upon winning, when she pointed upward and said, "He says I am beautiful!" No matter what others may have said, Candice celebrated in the truth that God calls her beautiful!!

From the time we enter the world, we start gaining knowledge that causes our armor to be tarnished. We wallow in filth and grime, and we roll around in mud and slime and engage in the slinging of muck. YET, despite the filth that we become covered in, the filth that often causes us to appear unrecognizable, even to ourselves, HE still calls us beautiful! Despite everything we do, or say, the people we get involved in, sins and the offenses we commit, He STILL says, "You're beautiful." What an awesome love that God must have for us, to see the ugliness that we are born into, but yet He loves us enough to say she is beautiful, he is beautiful. If the all-knowing God who sees us in the raw and still calls us beautiful, how dare we see and accept ourselves as anything less?

No matter how many babies a mother holds, or looks at, no baby is ever as beautiful as her own, and I dare anyone to contradict her on that fact! Even the mother of the worst serial killer calls that child beautiful. Why? Because he/she belongs to her!! Likewise, no matter what we do, or what mistakes we make, or how many times we pull away from Him, God STILL calls us beautiful. WHY? Simply because we belong to Him.

We are the ones whom He created, whom He called by name, and whom He died for!! How amazing is it that God sees beyond all the "stuff" and sees this beauty that He created! He looks beyond the black coal and sees the diamond. Marvin Sapp said it in a more creative way: *"He saw the best in me, when everyone all around could only see the worst in me."* ("He Saw The Best In Me", Marvin Sapp, Album: Here I Am, 2010) Another great artist, Dottie Rambo,(Album: Stand By The River 2003) went on to say, *"He looked beyond my fault and saw my need."* God looked beyond the stain and stench of sin to see the beauty in His masterpiece.

God calls us beautiful because He sees not what we are, but what He has created us to be! He's already declared that everything He does, and everything He created is good. In God's eyes, I am beautiful, I am good, and I am perfect! Through Him I am justified and qualified! So, with confidence and with Christ qualifying me to say so, I can stand boldly, despite the things I go through, and say with power and authority, "HE says I AM beautiful!!"

Chapter 57

Let's Be Honest

Sometimes, although I love God, I just don't care! What I mean is that sometimes there seems no difference in walking this life God's way and if there seems no difference then why not enjoy things doing it my way? Sometimes it seems like the world's way causes people to thrive, love, and be loved, but God's way only yields waiting and more waiting. And still, MORE WAITING!! Sometimes you get tired of crying because all your tears do is streak your face!

When my nights are lonely, my days are empty, and my heart screaming, for a moment I want to throw up my hands. This is especially when my press to do right, and to treat people with kindness; my desire to encourage and uplift seemingly yields ME, Andrea Beth Jenkins, absolutely NOTHING!! BUT, I so do love God! I want to be a woman that is different, a woman who in God's eyes stands out, a woman who in the eyes of someone special and in the eyes of those I come in contact with daily, mirrors the Christ I love and serve. I desire to be His spokesperson, His ambassador. Although in my flesh I want to do things Drea's way, I continue to press. I press through my tears, through my hurt, press through my unbelievable loneliness, press through frustration, and I press through responsibilities that I bear alone. I will continue to love on

God with all that I have; in my actions, and in my spirit, pushing, pressing, fighting and striving to be a woman of whom He can be proud. I want to be a woman, who brings a smile to His face, and a woman who, despite it all, desires more than anything to please Him.

Chapter 58

God Can Use Foolishness

I was lying in bed one night, unable to sleep, when a thought came to mind. Sometimes the foolishness we experience can be what reminds the devil that God is not a fool and can direct any situation for His honor!!

Without going into unnecessary detail, many of you who know me well, know some of the foolishness I dealt with at the hands of my son's biological father. This is by no means about bashing him, for at the end of the day I had a beautiful son with him and for that he will always have a level of respect and honor with me. This is solely about how God can use and change ANY circumstance so He can get glory! My son has a 19-year-old brother from a relationship his father had many years before me. I met this young man when he was four and never had much contact with him or his mother during my relationship. However, I would hear different things concerning her and while I heard them, I never fully digested them. Although I had connected myself to someone who was not divinely authorized, I still could discern some things. I knew that everything wasn't as it seemed, as I'm sure what was told to her concerning me wasn't all on the nose as well. One thing about me is that like to draw my own conclusions about things and people, and I try hard not to put an ending to a story unless I see it or experience it for myself.

A little over a year ago something prompted me to see if this young man was on Facebook, and that connection led me to his mother. In reaching out to her out of the common bond we shared, we developed a family relationship. Our sons were related by blood, and in developing our friendship I saw her strive to walk with God and we have been able to encourage each other both on a natural and spiritual standpoint. Recently she became ill and is battling cancer, and while we don't talk every day, I am in a place now where I can pray for her and encourage her! I read her posts and feel her struggle and know God used "foolishness" so that I could cover her in prayer and share a word of encouragement from time to time during this season.

The crazy paths we travel, whether God directed or self- directed can always be a path used to be a blessing to someone! Yesterday she posted a picture of herself without hair and in my spirit I wanted to embrace her and love on her because the beauty of God starts inwardly and radiates outward. Sometimes when we are in the middle of things, we don't know why we are in that place, but as we travel to the destination that God ultimately has for us, there are assignments along the way that have little to do with us but everything to do with serving and blessing others. As we bless others, we are blessed. Foolishness says we shouldn't even speak (and if truth be told, foolishness makes that true in a few areas) but God is no fool. What Satan will use to bring confusion, God will use to get glory!

Chapter 59

Superman -vs- Bizzaro

Romans 7:21 (NIV)
"So I find this law at work, Although I want to do good,
evil is right there with me."

Have you ever felt like you're living a "Spiritual Bizzaro" life, where everything is backwards, upside down and twisted? Superman was the hero, the heartthrob, the defender of all that was right. But because of a freak accident, Superman's exact opposite, Bizzaro, came and counteracted the essence of Superman. How often do we desire to do the things of God only to find ourselves doing the opposite? We desire to dispense mercy, but instead we judge. We want to fast, but we have the urge to try a new recipe.

We desire to sow into ministry, but we just have to get that new gadget or those new shoes. We want to go to worship, but the bed feels extra comfortable. We all are guilty of abiding in a spiritual Bizzaro world from time to time, gossiping when we should be covering, and giving into temptations when we should be fleeing from them. We are forever at war with ourselves, a battle between spirit and flesh. Often, we underestimate how strong, powerful and mighty the flesh is, and we feel that pure desire will keep us from those things that seek to trip us up, only to find ourselves digging out of the hole where we fell. The flesh yells and screams in our ears while blocking out the gentle whispers of the Spirit. The flesh forces itself upon us, while the Spirit behaves like a gentleman. The flesh can always justify its actions, while Spirit doesn't have anything to prove. So why do we accept being violated by the desires of flesh instead of yielding to the integrity of the Spirit?

Could it be because it's easier to give in than to wait for what God has for us? Is telling someone off easier then biting our tongue? Are we more inclined to believe that we deserve him or instead of having to endure waiting for the one God who selected for us? Thinking back on the things where I yielded, I can recall the conversations I had with myself. I wanted to please God, but I did not want to feel the discomfort associated with waiting on God. I was hearing myself in my head asking myself didn't I deserve some happiness but knowing this wasn't the way.

Have you ever seen a fight where the person who talks the most, shouts the loudest, provokes the most attention, talks the most trash is the one who gets beat to a pulp by someone less assuming? Louder doesn't always equal stronger or better; sometimes louder is just that - loud, hot air being expelled into the atmosphere. However, a soft whisper can command attention, and silence can hold more power. Peace has the ability to stop conflict in its tracks! If you think about the nature of God, never do we hear of Jesus speaking in a brash tone. His authority came in His ability to change circumstances in the whisper of His voice.

His whisper commanded attention. Satan uses tactics that will distract us from the calming voice of God, which causes to turn towards the source of the racket rather than to be guided by the gentleness of God. Bright lights, fireworks, flare guns draw attention; but candlelight, a small fire in the fireplace, a moonlit night brings about intimacy. So, the question becomes how do we stay away from a Bizzaro life in favor of a Christ driven life?

Although evil is around, how do we flee from it? In many ways that is an answer only answered by us individually, but for me, I would prefer to be wooed, romanced, and beckoned versus being pushed and violated. So, to focus on the gentleness that God is helping me drown out the temptations of Satan. Easy? Absolutely not, for even a woman who loves romance and likes to walk on the wild side every now and again. Knowing that what God offers me in the end will always outweigh what Satan has to offer, it helps me; and each of us must discover which characteristics of God helps to keep us. Waiting is hard, and watching others being blessed is hard. Its feeling like you are standing at the end of the line, but the awesome gifts that God has for me are much better than how I may feel now. So, I use the traits I love about myself, the traits that God has placed in me to keep me. I desire to live in the world of the spirit of God, rather in a world that is the opposite of what He has ordained for me.

Chapter 60

"i" Before "e" Except After "c"

ILOVE when God shows me something using the familiar!! "'i' before "e" accept after "c", or when sounding like "a", as in "neighbor" or "weigh"' The English language is filled with rules. Certain words are spelled or pronounced in certain ways in certain situations to meet our grammar structure, but then there are the "exceptions" to the rules, when something changes in order to accommodate certain circumstances!! God IS and will ALWAYS BE the exception to the rule. God often works outside of the box.

God is not typical, and when you think He's going to do something in a certain manner, it's NOT going to go that way. Not only can God NOT be pinned down to a certain way of doing things, He WON'T be pinned down! Rules infer that God is predictable, and while there are things we can hold God to, sticking to rules does not allow for God to do the impossible, to work a miracle, or to manifest the impossible. God wants us to experience Him in His fullness, and to allow Him to move and roam freely in our lives. We are to walk in expectation of God doing the impossible, but we must also walk in a way that allows Him the freedom and liberty to do for us in the manner in which He sees fit. With God working in our lives, it may seem easier doing so through the front door. But perhaps He desires to WOW us by coming through the window in the basement, or up through the slats in the floor. Imagine if limits had been placed on the colors of the rainbow, the wings of butterflies or the melodies of birds; the beauty of God we know now would not be known.

What I heard God say to me was for me not to limit what and how He chooses to work and move in my life. While there are ways He is known to work, I can't assume how He's going to work in my situation. Stand still and "see," observe how His hand will work. God has proven time and time again that He isn't a "typical" God. He will ask us to do things sometimes that don't make sense to us, but faith says that although situations look bizarre, when God has ordained something, we just need to LET Him do it. Allow Him to do what He does best in His unique way. Take the limits off God, unlock the handcuffs, saw off the chains and LET God be who He wants to be, and how He wants to be!

Chapter 61

An Intimate Love Affair

The core of God centers around one word, RELATIONSHIP. His desire is for us to have a close, intimate relationship with Him and for us to have close relationship with each other. The core of Satan is DIVISION. He wants to separate, break apart, and sever our relationship with God and sever relationships between people. Satan recognizes the strength and power that comes from unity. If you were to make a list of the things you desire in a marriage, you will find that many of those things are what God desires in the relationship He has with us.

We want someone to talk to, spend time with, someone who honors us, someone who will gush over us, and go over and above to make us happy. God desires the same in us. He wants to spend time with us, to talk and share our thoughts, dreams and concerns with Him. He wants to see the love we have for Him in action, and not just hear idle words. God wants to be the one whom we think about first thing in the morning, and the last person we think about at night. God wants to be in an intimate, loving relationship with us and He doesn't want to be second in our lives. The things we desire from the one we love didn't just pop into our minds. They were divinely planted in our spirits by a God shows us that exact type of love and who desires that same type of love in return.

Chapter 62

Collateral Blessings

{collateral damage (n) - Unintended damage, injuries, or deaths caused by an action, especially unintended civilian casualties caused by a military operation.}

All of us have experienced sadness when we hear of innocent people who were hurt or killed in war conditions or in connection to protesting causes. Nobody will soon forget 9/11. So many lives were lost and families devastated over a cause and the beliefs of a small group. We feel that weight and burden because people's lives were changed forever simply because they found themselves in situations where their only "offense" was being in the wrong place at the wrong time. They didn't do anything or say anything wrong, but were physically in an area targeted for trouble.

Earlier today God dropped into my spirit the thought of "Collateral Blessings." God is getting ready to cause blessings to fall upon people, not because of anything in particular they did or said, but simply because they have positioned themselves to stand close to God and to connect with those who are blessing carriers! Have you ever wondered why those of the Jewish faith are blessed, and why is it that whatever they touch flourishes? Although as a nation they denied Jesus, they were, still and will always be connected to

THE carrier of blessings, THE distributor of anointing! And anyone who aligns with them, or blesses them, will also find themselves in the path of blessings. There are some key people whom God has assigned to our lives who are blessing carriers. These are people who were assigned specifically to us to distribute blessings. But if we stray away from God, and if we dismiss people because of their outward packaging, we will miss out because we are not where we were supposed to be.

Think for a moment about the story of the seven foolish and seven wise virgins. All of them at one point were within radius of the bridegroom, and all of them were in line to receive a blessing simply because they were where they were supposed to be. But because of their lack of preparation, seven had to go outside of the perimeter, so that when the blessings were distributed they were not in place to be recipients of the collateral blessings. These were blessings that they hadn't done anything special to acquire, but blessings that they would have received just because they were in proximity.

God wants to drop spiritual atom bombs of blessings on His people, blessings that come to us just because we are connected to Him and to His ambassadors. But because we often stray, choose our own paths, or don't follow directions, we miss out on blessings that come from just standing still, and just being at Jesus' side. Whether we are being a blessing or covering to those who are blessing carriers, it is so important to be where God has placed you to be. You never know when God will dispense His blessings, His favor, or His anointing. Being close to God will always yield fruit, while being at a distance will always cause us to lose out on something special that He has in mind for those whom He loves.

Chapter 63

Canadian Geese

This morning I was laughing at a friend who commented that Canadian Geese were arrogant because they were holding up traffic walking across the highway. His comment had me thinking. Here are people are in cars that could easily run over the geese, but yet they will stop for them and let them pass. These geese will take their time and walk in front of a car without a care in the world, without even the remote fear that they could easily become roadkill. WOW!!

As children of God, we have to know who we are. As children of THE King, we have the right to walk with a spiritual arrogance! The size of our problems doesn't matter; the fact that situations could run us over doesn't matter. All that matters is that GOD is bigger than our issues! Because of this, we can walk without a care in the world!! We can walk as if nothing can destroy us, because at the end of the day while problems, issues, situations, hurts, may form, nothing that is formed can prosper. It can try, but it won't be successful!

Just like those geese, strutting across the highway, can cause cars that weigh tons to yield to their will; we can walk without fear too, knowing that at the name of Jesus, our situations have to yield and submit to the order of God. Geese know that the road belongs to them, and likewise we need to know that God has placed all of us on a path that leads to His divine will for our lives. We have been assigned to the road, so nothing that comes to run us over, side swipe us, or eliminate us has power! We have dominion, and thus like the Canadian Geese, can walk boldly knowing that nothing can overtake us as long as we remain submissive to the will of Him who owns the road!!

Chapter 64

Be Careful What You Pray For!

There are some feelings that are so engraved, so deeply tattooed in my spirit that my appreciation is so beyond what I asked God to place in me!!

What I'm experiencing is fueled by discomfort and other emotions, but in the midst of it I am soooooo grateful because God is doing the very thing I asked Him to do!!

BY NO MEANS DO I REGRET MY PETITION! Again, I am so very grateful! When you ask God for something that's very serious, be very careful, and make sure you know and understand exactly what you're asking Him to do. Why? Because when you ask God to do something within you, HOW He chooses to accomplish your request is 100% up to Him!!!

Chapter 65

I Don't Want What God Gave You!

When you enjoy, embrace and are comfortable in the lane God has called you to, you aren't likely to try to walk in and attempt to take over lanes that weren't assigned to you. If you embrace and enjoy being a woman/wife, you won't be so quick to take on the call, role and responsibilities of a man/husband. If you walk in and work to increase your gifts as a minister of Praise & Worship, an usher, a youth leader, or a deacon, you won't have time to walk in the role of the Pastor!! I enjoy the areas where God has called me.

I love being a woman, and I don't desire the role of a man. I will embrace the role of wife, and I will gladly submit to my head, my husband. I love being a mother, and I don't accept when people say I'm both mother AND father. While I understand their sentiments, I'm Rahjon's mother, and love it! I appreciate and treasure the gifts that God has given me, and I don't desire to acquire the gifts God gave to others. My gifts may not be like the gifts of others, but then, their gifts are not like mine ;)

When we embrace, accept and treasure the gems that God has given to each of us, we won't have time to desire the treasures of others because our focus will be on the precious things that God has placed uniquely within each of us.

Chapter 66

There Is A Time and Place For Everything

Everyone should have different aspects of their personalities, or different personas, where they can shift in and out of quickly at will. Some of those personalities may overlap, but other aspects are based on time and place. It is always funny to me when I'm in a store and I see one of my students. Young students don't always realize that teachers have homes and families; they tend to think that we live at school. So, when they see me, they almost go into shock!!

Being a teacher is only one aspect of who I am, and my students expect to see me in a certain light, I am a mother, a single mother at that, and there are certain things that my son should never see me do or hear me say. I am firm believers that while there are certain things that a child may hear or pick up at school, there are some things that a child should NEVER learn from their parents. My son knows of course that I am a woman, but what he sees is an aspect of my womanhood, and that aspect is being a mom. In church I am the worshiper, and a minister of praise. People see me on the choir, leading songs, and teaching music for Vacation Bible School. I may be involved in other ministry- related tasks, and while I enjoy worship, I enjoy those with whom I minister.

We have a good time together. At the same time, it's not the aspect of Andrea that is kickin' it with my friends, or the same person who is enjoying the church family day picnic with my close friends, or friends whom I have known all my life. I am more casual and lighthearted, and I'm quick to say something silly or out of the box. Within my community I carry myself in a way that represents WHO I belong to; I'm not loud, cussin', telling off cashiers, or screaming at my son, and acting less than a lady. In God's timing I desire and look to be a wife, and as a wife who I am at home in his private presence should not be the same wife that everybody else sees. There are aspects of my personality that are for ANYONE, aspects of my personality are for SOME, and then there is an aspect of my personality that is reserved for only THE ONE!!!

Sometimes we forget that people are always watching and observing. How do I know? How many times has someone walked past you and you noticed their shoes, hair, or bag? When a car comes down the street with music blaring, don't we look? If a child is having a temper tantrum in the store, don't we look to see how the parent is going to handle it? If we notice people, why wouldn't people notice us? It is with this thought that we have to be mindful of WHOM we represent and what aspect of our personalities we have on display at all times. A private wife persona should not be displayed anyplace but in front of a husband.

My parents instilled in me and were very serious on the concept of "TIME AND PLACE;" there is a time and place for everything, but the key is discerning if our actions are in alignment with the proper time and in the proper place. At the end of the day, we represent

Christ and we should always walk and conduct ourselves in a way that says we have good "Home Training," and good "God Training." If God isn't proud of us, if He isn't being represented correctly, and if our actions can be subject to question, then it's time to make a few changes or adjustments.

Chapter 67

The Butterfly Process

All of us want to skip the discomfort that comes with change, growth and elevation and get right to the good part. We go from A to Z without going through the letters in between. We KNOW that we can't become butterflies before we are caterpillars. KNOW that the transformation process takes place in the cocoon and that without the cocoon stage there is no transformation. We KNOW this, we understand this, and we get it!! BUT who likes pain? Who likes discomfort?

We KNOW what comes with transformation, and we KNOW it is a part of the process. And yet, out of our desire to be what God has called us to be, we go through it, although we wish we didn't have to! This is a place where I can personally relate. I KNOW the process, and I KNOW the reason for the process. I KNOW it's a must, and I KNOW that in the end when I come out that something great is in store. ALL OF THIS IS WHAT I KNOW, BUT flesh struggles with the discomfort of it all, although I KNOW He's working it out for my good! I KNOW what is coming is better than I could have imagined! So, what do I do? I will continue to trust God in the process and thank Him in advance for my Butterfly moment.

Chapter 68

The Best Gifts

The best gifts and the ones most treasured are the ones that are unexpected. If we remain open, and allow God to clear out the weeds in our lives, we will be blessed to experience blessings, gifts and surprises that ONLY God can give. God desires to give His children good things. These things are in the form of unexpected blessings, such as relationships that we never thought possible, and abundant opportunities that, by man's standards, we don't qualify for that God desires us to have. The same way that we as parents get a thrill when we're able to surprise our children with something they don't expect, Christ gets and enjoys a similar thrill when He surprises us with things we couldn't remotely anticipate!! Keeping ourselves open to the blessings, gifts and surprises of God will avail us to the awesome things that God wants to celebrate with us.

Chapter 69

THE FAITH OF ONE

> *I seek to see what you see, To discern what you discern,*
> *To listen to what you hear, To follow as you lead,*
> *To pray the prayers you pray,*
>
> *You are the head,*
> *I, a follower of your lead,*
> *Together we're the ONENESS God called us forth to be.*
> *(Anonymous)*

Marriage between a man and woman was designed to mirror the relationship we ought to have with Christ. We are the bride of Christ, the desire of His heart, the apple of His eye and thus ought to see what He sees, hear what He speaks, follow where He leads and pray those things which lines up with His will! When we become one with Christ, His desires become our desires, His characteristics become ours! We are one with Him, and our identity is that of Him! This poem illustrates the desire I have to be a wife to the husband of whom I am waiting for God to bless me, but in a deeper form. We should all have the same desires as the bride of Christ.

Chapter 70

Mirror, Mirror On The Wall

The Disney story of *Snow White and the Seven Dwarfs* is based on the concept of what can happen when someone gets consumed with the gifts of someone else and allows their desire to sabotage someone else. In the story, the queen was happy and content until an inquiry from her mirror gave her a response she was not anticipating. The mirror indicated that someone else was more "gifted" than she, which had her seeking to destroy the young Snow White.

When we become disenchanted with the gifts and talents that God gave us and we seek to have the gifts God gave to another, then we are no longer effective vessels. Each of us are given gifts and talents based on those whom God has assigned to our lives. If we seek to have what belongs to another, then those placed in our charge now are uncovered and we are held accountable. There are specific people who have to read your book, heard your testimony, or meditated on your song, but if because you are focused on the gift of someone else you fail to write, tell or sing then those waiting for the seeds that you have to plant in them are now ineffective and can't move forward in their assignments, which also affect the growth of others! Your gift is important to the body of Christ; it is assigned to you based on what God has placed within you, and not what has been placed in others. God gifted you! God equipped you! God anointed you to complete a task, so walk in YOUR assignment with the tools that YOU'VE been given and do what God has called YOU, and only YOU, to do.

Chapter 71

The Road Traveled

Some years ago, I had a dream that was separated into two parts. In the first part, God showed me the route HE had mapped out for me, the stops along the way and the ending point. In the second part God showed me the path I ACTUALLY took, the stops along the way and the ending point. The path that God intended for me to take was smoother, less difficult, and involved fewer tears, while the route I took was bumpy, and a lot of things that took place didn't have to happen and involved more hurt and tears. But the common thread between the two avenues was that my ending point was the same!

How I got there was different, but the end result was the same! I share that to say this: even when we do things that cause our life to go off course, or when things happen that are not within our control lands us in territory we don't recognize, the grace of God steps in and still allows us to end up where He intends us to be. It's like going on a planned trip by plane and due to mechanical problems we can't take a plane but we take Amtrak instead. The trip is longer, not as comfortable, the scenery is different BUT the destination is the same.

Today I want to encourage you. Your destination never changed; just the way you're traveling to get there, and while the "A" plan has changed, God can manipulate the other 25 letters in your favor! The "Z" plan lands you in the same spot as the "A" plan would have taken you! Our destinations change when we decide to halt the trip altogether. Our travel plans may be altered, but when we choose to keep on moving, God steps in as our travel agent and He makes the changes that allow us to get to our final destination. And, even if the path is not as smooth or comfortable, God still buffers us so that we still don't feel the full brunt of all the potholes that tend to be on back road trails. That is the beauty of God's grace and mercy; when things in our lives shift and change, GOD still keeps us on course!!

Chapter 72

Who Represents You?

Recently I was introduced to someone with whom I will work/minister closely, the person was polite, but quiet and reserved. When I would see this person in passing during the week, they would smile say hello but not much else. I understood the quietness because I am like that; I'm very much shy and reserved until I get to know you, so their quiet demeanor didn't offend me. So fast forward, I was invited to a celebration for someone I am VERY close to, someone who God has allowed both of us to be there together for over several years.

This new acquaintance, who was also invited, came in. I could see that they were taking note of who was a part of this small gathering. It was less than 15 people, and they were still quiet and reserved but I noted that they had taken mental notes. Fast forward again, I ran into this person today and you would have thought that we had known each other forever! We were talking and joking; they were completely at ease talking with me. It was at that point that two things dropped into my heart and spirit. The company you keep really does matter, and whom you associate with speaks to who you are. As a child, my dad drilled that concept into my sister and me: "Watch the company you keep!!"

As I was thinking about the encounter, I reflected on the point that although the person was friendly, they didn't know me and wasn't familiar with my character, so they were cautious. Mmmm!! I respect that. Once they became aware that I was a part of this intimate circle, they felt comfortable enough to embrace a new friendship. We should all take that stance. We need to be aware of whom we connect to, because our association represents them and, in turn; their association with us represents us. In this situation, I didn't have to say a word; the company I was with spoke to the type of person that I was and what I stood for. It was a powerful lesson.

We can't connect and attach ourselves to everybody. Our witness is less about what we say out of our mouths, and more about what we speak via our actions and the actions of those to whom we are attached. As much as people wanted to attach themselves to Jesus, His inner circle was small. Although He made Himself available to everyone, Jesus knew He couldn't be connected to everyone. He took the time serve everyone who desired His service. If Jesus was mindful of HIS connections as a representative of God, how much more should we be mindful of our connections and ourselves as we strive to be representatives of Him as well.

Chapter 73

Gilligan's Island

How does a three-hour tour turn into spending years on an island? How does a short journey from Egypt turn into a forty-year journey? How does the path we walk turn into years of walking? Could it be that there is something in us that is causing a delay? Could it be that sometimes we prolong our own journey? There are times in life where God takes us the long way to strip away, plant and restore some things. Sometimes He prolongs our manifestation so that when we get it we are in a place not only to handle it, but we also can maintain it! Then, there are times when our manifestation is delayed due to our own decisions. We take our own path and listen to advice that is not God given, or we're in pride and we think that we know the path better than God!

When things are delayed or prolonged in our lives, it is important to pause and take stock of what is happening. Is the delay due to God working within us, or is it due to our own actions? The children of Egypt were delayed from entering the Promised Land due to disobedience. God was not going to allow a hardheaded bunch of people to enter into a new season when they were not grateful enough to Him for delivering them from their oppressors. So, God waited for that generation to die off before he allowed them to enter in. You can't walk into a new season with the attitudes of the prior season.

Now in the case of Abraham, it looked like the promise would never come. He and his wife were old, and naturally past their childbearing years. It seemed like time was not on their side. But the question was, did they trust God? Would they believe God for their manifestation, despite how it looked? Although they made mistakes, God still maintained His promise to them, but they had to wait another 14 years after Ishmael was born before Isaac, THE promise was born. The delay was a question, a test. Do You Trust Me? Do you believe I will do what I said I'd do? The delay was to strengthen their trust in God and strip away doubt.

Can you discern your delays? Are you being delayed as a way to mature you, or are you being delayed because your life is not lining up with the will of God? Do you seek to know the difference? If God has you on delay to create in you what He desires you to be, then know that when manifestation comes it will be greater than the time spent on delay. But if your delay is due to your life needing to be modified, then God is giving you to time to get yourself together. Delay does not have to be the end; it could be the beginning of newness in Christ or the re-establishing of your life.

Chapter 74

Eenie Meenie Miney Mo. Which Way Jesus Shall I Go?

There are times when we simply don't know what to do. We seek, we listen, and we pray; but we get nothing. Sometimes we feel that maybe we should roll some dice, or like we did as kids play Eenie, Meenie, Miney Mo and randomly pick a direction. Our minds can be so cluttered that we can't hear. When this happens, we have to learn to settle our spirits down and listen. We need to meditate and tune our ears to the still, calming voice of God.

When the children of Israel saw that Pharaoh's army was coming after them and that there was no place to go with the Red Sea in front of them, they began to panic. But look at what Moses tells them; he said, "Stand still and see the goodness of The Lord." (Scripture Reference) In other words, calm down and watch God. Life can keep us in a frantic, panic-like state, but God wants us to calm down and see what He will do. Listen to what He is saying, and allow Him to direct our choices. When we come to those forks in the road and we don't know what to do or which way to go, that is not the time to play Russian Roulette with our future. Instead, it's time to find our meditation closet and simply be still and allow God to minister to our spirits. He is waiting at the crossroads, but often in the hustle and bustle we don't even see Him, then we make choices that are to our detriment. If you have ever gone on a road trip, often along the highway there are rest stops, where you can take a breather from driving and rejuvenate. God wants us to receive what He has for us at His spiritual rest stop to gain rest, to gain direction, and to regain our strength before continuing on our journey. Don't be so quick to make choices when you're not sure. Take time to be still and to hear what the Spirit is saying to you.

Chapter 75

Hit Me With Your Best Shot! Fire Away!

In the early 80's, Pat Benatar sang a song entitled, "Hit Me With Your Best Shot." (Written by: Eddie Schwartz, Album: Prisoner of Love, 1980) One of the verses says ...

"You come on with a come on, you don't fight fair, but that's O.K., see if I care! Knock me down, it's all in vain, I'll get right back on my feet again! Hit Me with your best shot! Why Don't You Hit Me With Your Best Shot! Hit Me With Your Best Shot! Fire Away!"

Oftentimes we spend a lot of time ducking the devil, complaining about the devil, and rebuking the devil while forgetting that God has given us the power to defeat the devil! When you know you are equipped for something, and there's no reason to run, you stand up and fight through your situations, knowing that God has given you what you need to win!! Yes, the devil has weapons, but so do we! Yes, the devil is strong, but greater is He that is within us! Yes, the devil has developed weapons to destroy us, but the word says that no weapons formed against us shall prosper. We serve a mighty God, and while every battle isn't ours to fight, God wouldn't tell us to put on the whole armor if there wasn't going to be some fighting now and again. So even when we are called to fight, even if we do get knocked around a bit, and even if we get a little bruised, we have the backing of Christ that allows us to stand tall and firm and face what comes our way. We can tell the devil to give it his best shot, because in the end we know the devil is already defeated. As the children of God, we have the victory. God will be exalted!

Chapter 76

REVELATION

Satan can't destroy what God creates! He can shift it, shake it up, or rearrange it, but destroy it? ABSOLUTELY NOT! It's not within his power. God's ultimate purpose will be manifested in the end.

An original plan may have taken a detour, BUT God's ultimate plan for your life can never be destroyed. So with this in mind, we can stand firm in the midst of earth's tremors. We can stand, knowing that the purpose for which God created us, and the things He created to bless our lives cannot be destroyed. The abilities of God will always supersede the abilities of Satan! Satan's powers are scarce when compared to the Almighty power of God.

So, stand through the crashing of waves; God will not let you drown. Stand, and when the wind causes you to bend, God will not allow you to break. Stand, and when your legs feel shaky, God will not allow you to crumble. Satan destroys, but God builds. Satan kills, but God brings life and life more abundantly. Satan wants to see you fail, but God wants you to thrive! Satan wants your death, but God wants your resurrection! Whose report will you stand on? The One who creates life or the one who, despite his limited power, wants to destroy it?

Chapter 77

Your Way? Or GOD's Way?

Sometimes we have images in our minds of how things "should" look, and we have preconceived ideas as to "how" God is going to do something.

When we lock onto those thoughts, it can be difficult for us to see what and how God is "actually" going to do something. We put God in a box and don't allow Him the opportunity to manifest a miracle. We must rid ourselves of what WE think and be open to who, what and how of God's plan so we can have what God desires for us. Our image may be good, but God doesn't want us to have just good. God wants to blow our minds. For Him to do that, He has work through unexpected events, things we never thought about, or don't think will work. That person we didn't anticipate, that move we didn't plan on, that friendship we weren't looking for: Don't tie God's hands! Let Him be free to do the unexpected!

Chapter 78

Just To Be Close To You

When you are in a relationship with someone, trouble will arise if one strays too far from the other. This is not just physically, but mentally. A husband and wife become one and should function as one. When there is a spiritual separation between them, the entire relationship will begin to crumble because one unit is operating independently.

Lesson One: Couples need to work to maintain oneness. He can't allow her to stray too far, and she must seek to keep her stance in close proximity to his. This applies spiritually and naturally.

Lesson Two: Likewise, as the bride of Christ, we have to work to maintain our oneness with God. We should always check to see where we are in relationship to where He is! God is always calling us, and He desires us to be close to Him but sometimes we stray too far and can't hear Him calling. Our position should never be to where we are out of the earshot of God. In the same way that He desires us to be close to Him, we ought to work hard to keep Him close. It's not a one-way relationship. If God calls out to us constantly, and desires us to be close to Him, then we ought to be calling out to Him while desiring that He will always be close to us.

NOTE: I have found that the things I desire in my future husband are things God wants from me as well. That includes Intimacy, Communication, Love, Affirmation, Loyalty, Faithfulness, etc.! I have to give to God and my future spouse those things that I desire for myself!!

You can't be intimate with someone if there is no closeness! Intimacy is deeper than surface or physical affection. Being intimate allows you to feel someone's presence, even if they are not near you physically.

{Intimacy = A Deeper Level of Discernment}

Being close to God requires me to be intimate with Him.

Chapter 79

Now I'm Giving Back To You

Rev. Milton Brunson sang a song titled, "I'm Available to You."("I'm Available To You", Written by Rev. Milton Brunson, 1988) Here is one of the verses and the chorus:

VERSE:

Now I'm giving back to You all the tools You gave to me,

My hands, my ears, my voice, my eyes; so You can use them as You please.

I have emptied out my cup, So that You can fill me up Now I'm free and I just want to be more available to You.

CHORUS:

Lord I'm available to You. My will I give to You. I'll do what You say do. Use me Lord

To show someone the way, and enable me to say My storage is empty, and I am available to You.

When you give back to God the gift(s) He gave to you and you're serious about allowing Him to use you in the area of your gift(s), He will do amazing things through your gift(s) and show Himself in amazing ways. All God requires from us is that we make ourselves available to Him, that we be willing vessels, that we allow ourselves to be pliable, moldable, and flexible!! When we allow God to manipulate us as He pleases, then people are blessed, and lives are changed.

Growing up there was a song they use to sing (often at offering time, lol) that said, *"If you give unto The Lord, He will give you more to give."* When we give of ourselves to God willingly, He will pour more into us to give out to others. *"The more He gives, the more He gives to you, just keep on giving, because His word is true. You can't, beat God giving, no matter how you try."*

"I give myself away so You can use me" Our gifts are not so we are glorified. Although God does allow room for some appreciation, our gifts are so that people will come to know the love that Christ wants to offer them. We should use our gifts in a way that reaches people on their level.

Chapter 80

Growth and Development

O ne of the things I may review in my (our) students is their fine motor skill level. Fine motor skills demonstrates their ability to manipulate small objects, how they hold their pencils, eating utensils, how they work their buttons, belts, zippers and so on. One of the things we do during evaluations is to give students small blocks and challenge then to build a tower as high as they can without it falling over. Students are given a few opportunities to accomplish this goal. As I am growing and maturing in God, I see Him giving me opportunities to "stack my blocks;" I have opportunities to work on my balance, and handle challenges that will strengthen the areas where I may not be as strong. While the blocks still tumble at times, those times are decreasing. Areas that I didn't handle well in the past, I now handle better. Things that made me dissolve in tears in the past; I may now require a facial tissue only occasionally.

I am not where I was, and I'm not where I will be,
but I'm grateful for how far I've come, and where I am now!

Chapter 81

Residue

Here's a question to ask yourself: What kind of residue are you leaving in the lives of those to whom you are connected? When you leave someplace or when there is a relationship shift, the atmosphere should be better than before you entered! Those to whom you are connected, whether short or long term, should be better because of what you deposited into their lives. It's hard to get rid of residue; it's a type of film that adheres strongly to something. You have to apply some elbow grease to get rid of it.

So the question we must ask ourselves is this: Are we leaving a positive or negative residue? When people think about you, do the seeds, words or wisdom and encouragement you've left continue to marinate and add to someone's growth? Or is what you left behind a source of hurt that they now have to work hard to recover from? This is just a little something to think about and consider.

Chapter 82

God's Compassion

I'm thinking about how Jesus handled sin. He rebuked, He chastised, and He corrected, but He also showed compassion! I remember my greatest fall in my 20's and what took place. What stands out the most in my mind about that time in my life is how God handled my situation. On the Sunday following my fall I opted not to sing with the choir so that I could get my head straight and re- establish myself.

On this Sunday the spirit was high, and people were called to the altar to be prayed for and receive a Word. I took this opportunity to also come to the altar and as I stood there pouring myself out to The Lord, I heard the spirit almost audibly say three simple words, *"You are forgiven."* I recall how overwhelmed I was with emotion, and how I couldn't believe what I had just heard! Only a few days had gone by, and what had taken place was huge. But yet, I was forgiven! The voice of God was sooo clear that when I looked up, the person next to me said to me, *"Did you hear that?"* so I knew that God had spoken! God looked at me, not in light of my sin, but despite it!! My forgiveness, rebirth, and restoration came through my worship and service, and through the compassion of God.

Chapter 83

He Wants It All

God is holistic. He is concerned about the spiritual and the natural aspects of our lives. He desires to see us prosper in every aspect of our lives, from our relationship with a Him, to our relationship with others! God looks at our spiritual purpose and our earthly purpose. He looks at our worship and our weight, and our calling and careers.

God wants to be a part of all of it! Our victories and our failures; and our excitement and times of procrastination – God still wants to be part of all of it. We must learn to commit every aspect of our lives to God! Our issues, our insecurities, and our triumphs – He cares about all of it. As the song says, *"He wants it all."* God wants to build us up where we are weak, and help us move even further where we are strong. The key is not to pick and choose what we turn over to God, but to submit everything to Him.

Lord, You know every aspect of me: my strengths, my weaknesses, and the things I am proud of, and the areas where I am insecure. You know the areas where I jump to accomplish and the areas where I procrastinate. So I submit my all to You! I offer to You the good, the bad, and the ugly. I lay it all at Your feet. I submit the spiritual side of Andrea as well as the natural side; unite both aspects of me so I can be what You desire of me.

Chapter 84

Going Against the Grain

Sometimes, for us to fulfill our purpose in God, He will have us operate in ways that are out of the norm, or out of the realm of what the world has labeled as standard operating practice. God is moving us against the grain, and against what's natural in order to accomplish something supernatural in our lives!! WOW!!

So now the question becomes WHY does God do this? Why does He need to deal with us through unconventional methods? Why does God take us through the back door, down the side streets, and through the jungle instead of the most direct and fastest route? The reason is very simple; God wants to stand out in our lives. He wants to make a life lasting impression. He wants us to remember what it took to get from where we are to where He's taking us! There are lessons to be learned; wisdom to be obtained, and testimonies to be birthed. Those things come through God leading us through channels that are not typical.

As I think on this topic I am reminded of various icons in the Bible whom God led through the back entrance to teach lessons and minister the greatness of God. The prophet Hosea who God told to take a prostitute as his wife: WHAT?! God commanded His servant to take a wife who would continue to dishonor him, who would embarrass him, and who he would have to retrieve from the beds of other men! Huh!? But in doing so, God taught a lesson on his undying love for us. No matter how much we dishonor him, shame him, turn away from him, or consort with others, He will continue to seek us and desire us back!! I think about David.

While God knew he would commit adultery and then murder, He still went against the grain by choosing someone who was not of the royal house if Saul; a shepherd to lead the children of Israel. Again, God went against the grain by making Solomon David's heir to the throne instead of Absalom, David's first born. There is Mary, a virgin, whom God led down the path to be the mother of Jesus, which was clearly against the grain!! Joseph was lead down a path of betrayal, lies and prison before his purpose was manifested!

Often, we don't know why we are on the road that we travel, and why we have to wait on things while others seem to get their desires handed to them on a silver platter. Sometimes we get tired of the struggle, the tests, and the tears; we become annoyed and frustrated with the process and honestly want to throw up our hands and just forget it. We ask ourselves, *'is all this worth it?'* The word of God answers this question for us when it says, "Weeping may endure for a night, but joy cometh in the morning." Yes, it is hard now! And yes, the tears still flow. Yes, we continue to question, but the call on our lives and the harvest that will come from our journey will allow those whom God has connected to us to meet their mandate!!

Years ago, there was a commercial for the shampoo Prell. It showed two people telling two others about the product, who in turn tell two more friends, who told two friends, and so on. What we experience is not about just us, but those two who tell two, who tell two, who then tell two!! Our going against the grain experience is for the masses!! So don't give up! Continue to let your hair be brushed the "wrong" way, your grass to be mowed in the "opposite" direction, and for your car to drive in the opposite direction down a "one way" street!! God sees the outcome. And while we may feel we are walking in the wrong direction, anything that God orchestrates is always the right way. Backward to us, is forward to God! Wrong to us is right to God! Our job is to trust Him and follow Him, knowing that even when He is leading us through a "backwards" territory, in the end it will all align correctly when God calls us forth!

Chapter 85

Choose Your Team Wisely

Looking at my family and friends, my "team lineup:" those who start, those who are on the bench but cheering, and those hanging out in the locker room waiting for champagne bottles to be popped. It is the desire that this organization will move forward in the spiritual game while performing at its highest level. Because of this, players need to be cut! It makes no sense to have players on the team that don't add to the overall strength of the organization.

Every player is not a good match on every team, and to stay at peak performance, there must be a good fit. It doesn't necessarily mean that they are bad players; it could just mean that they don't have the specialized skills needed for where your team wants and needs to go! Having a good player in an organization doesn't guarantee a championship. And what team doesn't play to win?! As a player on assigned teams, I desire to give it my all!, I play so they can win!!, it's my objective to encourage, sow, support and work hard, and assisting so that the teams I'm divinely connected to can obtain their spiritual "championship rings."

There is a danger in playing and toying around with the lives of God's people! If I am not a good teammate, then I'm not showing good spiritual sportsmanship!! So likewise, as I seek my own championship ring, I look for those on my team to play similarly as to how I play! I play hard to win, and I do so with integrity!! And since God has given me the assignment, it's up to me to choose who is on my team!! Ahhhh Yes! As I look at my team, it's time to cut and draft some folks!!

The players on your team are those that surround you, and those who are in your circle. All who are in your personal space is totally up to you! If they don't add to your life, they don't deserve the honor of being on your team!

CHOOSE YOUR TEAM WISELY!!

Chapter 86

The Divorce Was Sent to Bless

Here's an observation: The disrespect of Queen Vashti towards the King, her husband, resulted in the King "divorcing" her. The separation allowed God to manipulate circumstances to crown Esther as Queen. She found favor with the King, who in return saved God's people from destruction!!

Lesson: Sometimes there is more favor in being second instead of first.

Lesson: At times God will cause a separation or "divorce" to take place to establish whom He desires!

Lesson: Sometimes we lose things, lose people, and some have experienced divorce and other forms of deep hurt; but God is able to restore!

What God will bless you with after you experience heartache; will be more precious than what you had in the past. The latter will be greater!! We don't have to feel used up or like second-hand goods; God has something special for us that could only come by way of shedding, or the separation from the past. You are not tainted or damaged!! God just has to prepare the way for you to come forth and for the heart you will touch and bless!!

Chapter 87

Bend, Don't Break

Have you ever heard of a car accident involving a drunk driver where the person in the other car was killed, but the drunk driver survived? Ever wonder why that is? When a person is not in control of their body upon an impact, the body goes with the direction and flow of the vehicle. However, if you are aware that there is going to be an impact, you'll tighten up your body, which causes it to go against the directional flow. Thus, upon impact, if the body is resisting, it causes a thrust of the body, which results in damage and possibly death. The body went against the natural flow.

Often as we travel through storms in our lives, our natural response is to brace ourselves, become rigid, and to buck and fight against the pressure. Fighting against the pruning season and against God's desire to refine us only causes us more pain and anguish! Instead of fighting against God, the best way to get through our situations is to flow with God! Due to the effects that alcohol can have on the body, a person in that state is flowing with the current of the car. If we consume ourselves with the things of God and focus on His purpose for our lives instead of fighting against the process, we will find that we are more flexible, bendable, and the bumps that come with perfecting us won't hurt as much.

Fighting against God NEVER works but flowing with Him allows us to go through the process in such a way that brings a greater victory. If we must go through, why do so in a way that causes more hurt, harm and damage? Consume yourself with God and allow yourself to become drunk in His presence. Although the process of refining may not be easy, it can be smoother. It's our choice in how we want to travel.

Chapter 88

There's A Reason For the "Error"

A delay, a denial, a rejection, something was missed, broken, or accidentally thrown away; maybe a wrong number, clerical error, too much of this, too little of that, wrong exit, missed turn, overqualified, or underqualified - all of these seem like examples of errors, of things that seemingly went wrong. But are they really? The wrong turn may have caused you to miss an accident; the overqualified response allowed you to accept a better position, and the rejection allowed you to meet your assigned Boaz or Ruth. God never allows things to happen without a purpose! What seems like a mistake is in reality a way for Him to bless us beyond what we would be willing to accept, or an opportunity to be a blessing to someone else.

I was speaking to a friend earlier who shared with me an "error" that the Post Office made. A letter with a very similar street address but from an entirely different state was put in her P.O. Box by "mistake." The letter looked important, so my friend opted to see if the addressee was on Facebook. She sent an inbox message explaining the "error," and she told them that she was praying for them based on the contents of the letter. Now we don't know what the letter was about, nor is that important, but God opened an opportunity by way of an "error" for someone to know that God has them in mind through prayer!

God is quick to manipulate situations and circumstances for HIS purpose! In God there are no mistakes, only opportunities and chances to bless and favor us and to use us to reach others! Mistakes and errors can't always be looked at as such. When things happen, the question we need to ask God is, "How do You want to use this for Your glory?" Or "God, how are You going to manipulate this "error" for my good?"

Chapter 89

Let Go But Don't Give Up

S ometimes life may require you to "Let Go" of some things or some people. Letting go frees you up for what God has for you. While it may behoove you to "Let Go," it is never in our favor to "Give Up." Letting go allows God to give something better, but giving up denotes the loss of hope, and the loss of faith. Giving up ties the hands of God, because it says you don't believe in His ability to change your circumstances. Let go of the past, but don't give up on your future. Let go of your pain, but don't give up on restoration. Let go of what he/she did to you, but don't give up on believing that God has someone special just for you! Let go of things that can hinder your growth in God, but never give up on believing that God's working everything out for your good.

Chapter 90

World Series Champions

The 2013 Red Sox's World Series win serves as an important reminder. Being in last place with everything "seemingly" against you isn't the final word, or the last say in your life. Your condition and your past don't have to be permanent. God is able and has the ability to catapult you from where you are right into first place! It can happen in the blink of an eye!! You may have lost a lot of battles or did not do what God directed you to do, but your past does not dictate your future. Your issues are written in spiritual pencil. Only God holds the permanent pen to which your future is written. With the favor of God, you have the ability to take it all!! Don't let the past keep you from what God has declared for your future!

Chapter 91

Changing Andrea

In this season of being single I have learned so much! One of the major things I have learned is to look less at the other half of the relationship, and focus on my half of the relationship instead. Nobody owns 100% of the issues within a relationship! Everyone has a stake in what takes place, even if your portion was as "little" or as "minor" as giving someone the silent treatment. Instead of looking at what "they" did and judging their actions, I have learned to look at Andrea, and to take ownership for the areas of weakness that I have and make a deliberate effort to work on them.

When a teacher gives a makeup exam, she never gives it directly after returning a failing grade to a student, but instead she gives the student ample time to review their errors and study for the new test. God is no different; when we fail, or fall short, God will give us the time to work on ourselves, to improve ourselves and to learn better ways to handle those things that caused us problems. God wants us to succeed, so instead of looking at the errors of those with whom we were in relationships, the best thing we can do is deal with the person in the mirror so that when God gives us another opportunity, we are equipped, more disciplined and ready to walk into our new relationship with victory. It won't be perfect, but when you have the necessary tool and weapons, you are better able to handle the various things that seek to destroy the new blessing that God has gifted you.

When we choose to work on us to be the best half of a relationship that we can be, God honors us by giving us new blessings and new chances to enjoy a fresh relationship and a fresh covenant! While by no means do I claim perfection, the lessons I have learned, and the wisdom that has been deposited into me, as well as the areas that I've tried to improve over the last several years of being single have prepared me to be a better friend, partner, wife then I ever was in the past. I can be transparent with me and acknowledge my areas of weakness because I desire that second chance and want to present to someone an Andrea that is divinely new and improved!

Chapter 92

Your "HOW" Is Just As Important As Your "WHAT"

G od had been dropping this in my spirit for several weeks, but while I didn't speak on it until later, I kept hearing it. God is protective of His people. He may allow things to happen to stretch us, mature us and promote growth in Him. God will not allow Satan to mess with us, and there is a cost to those who mess with those who God calls His own. With that being said, we must be very careful how we speak and handle people! Even on our admonishing, correcting and teaching there is a way we must handle God's people.

There is a danger in bullying. There is a danger in hurting others, and there is a danger in self-righteous attitudes. When handling the people God calls His own, the Fruit of the Spirit must apply: love, joy, a peaceful approach, exceeding patience with people, showing kindness, addressing issues with gentleness, and handling concerns with Godly self-control and with a spirit of meek and humility. Often it is not the "WHAT" that hurts and damages people, but the "HOW," the approach. And, even if what we say is correct, God is concerned about how we treat others! The Word reminds us to not let our good be evil spoken of. When God has gifted us to sow into people, we cannot allow the good, the wisdom, and the lessons to be tainted because the approach one chooses to address people is laced in arrogance and painted in condescending comments or draped in judgment. Yes, the Word must be delivered honestly and not watered down, but with all the words available to us with just the English language alone, we ought to be able to share the truth of God without further damage.

People many leave convicted to change course by our words, but our words should never leave someone wounded because we made the choice not to use words that are specifically designed to up build up and empower others. Presentation is everything! If you go to a restaurant the food "could" be delicious, and the chef "could" be the best in the world, but if he just slops the food on the plate and it looks nasty, how good it is won't matter if no one eats it. HOW something is presented is just as important as WHAT'S being presented!!

Chapter 93

God Sees

One of my Facebook friends shared her desire for a particular kitchen mixer. This woman of God is very gifted in cooking all kinds of awesome things for her family, things that don't include the calories, sugar, additives and preservatives of commercial food. She needed a mixer that would endure her culinary creations. Now let me give you a bit more insight into my friend; she is the wife of a pastor and has four young children. My friend is the epitome of a Proverbs wife and mother. Her family IS her ministry and through the vehicle of her husband and family her worship to God reached the throne.

Now let's talk about the awesomeness of God. This mixer that my friend desired had a price tag of $300.00 but it was her desire to have it. Not even a week after sharing her desire for this mixer with her husband and posting a picture on Facebook, did a FedEx package arrive at her door from an unknown source. Can you guess what was in the box? If you guessed a brand-new mixer, the one she desired, with all the attachments, you are absolutely correct! As she shared her appreciation, her excitement, and her GRATEFULNESS to God and to the unknown giver of the gift, God placed in my spirit how He showed her favor because He accepts the worship, she gives Him through honoring and serving her family. God sees her and sees all that she is doing to worship Him!!

Friends, GOD SEES US!! As the people in whom God delights, He wants us to be reminded that He DOES see us! He sees our efforts; He sees our push, and He sees our striving. He sees our tears, He sees our sweat, He sees our determination, and He sees our press. He sees our love for Him. Now *our* view of things might be hazy at times, but God has the ability to see us through the haze. Know and be encouraged that God DOES see you, and based on what He sees, he is preparing something special and exclusively for you! Continue to give Him your worship through the vehicle that He used to favor you; continue to give Him your offering of praise. Don't become weary as you walk through the fog of life! He sees you; you're in His scope of vision! Nothing you do is unseen by God, and no form of worship goes unacknowledged. If you continue to be faithful with your worship, God will honor you and allow YOU to see that He has seen!

Chapter 94

Are Your Spiritual Bones Set Correctly?

If you break a bone and it is not set right, it will heal, but heal incorrectly. It's not enough to "just" be healed from our past hurts and issues; we must seek to be healed correctly. A bone that heals incorrectly can cause a limp, crippling, and pain in the future and we won't be able to function as God has called and ordained us. A bone that heals incorrectly will have to be broken again and reset so that it can function as it was designed.

Many people are walking around claiming they have been healed from their past, but in reality they have healed incorrectly, thus they are not functioning at the capacity that God has called us. Bones that have not been properly set can result in attitudes and behaviors that do not represent the divine healing of God's hand.

When you have experienced God's divine healing, then bitterness, a spirit of judgment, a lack of compassion, and a lack of grace and mercy will not be a part of your disposition. You speak life. You don't degrade; you encourage. You don't seek to bring people down; your arm of correction also has a hand of mercy at the end of it. Divine healing is a process that takes place internally and expressed openly.

Chapter 95

The Loving Hand Of A Shepherd

Just a thought: People need to be treated with MORE compassion and LESS punishment.. God is a God of correction, but His hand of grace, mercy and compassion is dispensed MORE than His hand of anger! And never does God belittle people while teaching and guiding them!

I believe in the COMPASSION of God, and the MERCY of God and the GRACE of God! These are HUGE aspects of the ministry of Jesus. He was sent to earth to die as an act of love and compassion. Yes, there are times when we will receive the hard hand of correction, which is the hardness of His love. BUT even then, it often comes only after a lot of grace and mercy and often comes as a result of hardheadedness. As parents, more often we dispense grace, mercy and compassion to our children. The times of punishment and the hard hand of parenting are far outweighed by our gentle hand. Likewise, God chooses to handle us in the same manner.

Let's take a moment to reflect over the time when Jesus was serving people. How often was his anger kindled? How often did He come down with the gavel? Did He ever belittle, embarrass, or insult people? Did He ever appear superior in His teaching, even though He was superior? A Shepherd is not harsh towards the sheep.

He understands the mentality of the sheep and handles them with loving care. There are some animals you have to beat down, but not sheep. God clearly calls us His sheep and refers to Himself as a loving Shepherd.

Some people are shepherds; others are lion tamers. God calls us sheep, so based on that description, it would seem to reason that God prefers the person who walks in the spirit of a Shepherd, rather than the person who walks in the spirit of a lion tamer.

Chapter 96

Household Maintenance

No matter how grand the house, or how much it costs, or how much it takes to furnish it; at some point the wood floors will need to be redone, the walls painted, the tiles replaced, and the security system needs to be updated. These things are done periodically as part of the responsibilities of a homeowner in maintaining their home. Our spiritual homes/temples require the same regular upkeep and maintenance. We must check corners for dust and cobwebs check, for grout in-between our tiles, defrost and wipe out the refrigerator, and throwing away expired food.

Smoke detectors must be checked, and batteries changed; air filters and light bulbs must be replaced, and the list goes on. We can't allow our spiritual homes to deteriorate! We must be concerned consistently with our spiritual upkeep. When you let things go, or put things off for later, it becomes easy to fall into a state of spiritual laziness and negative contentment. Take care of your temple, and safeguard it against the storms of life. Stay on top of it, and don't take small cracks and tiny fractures lightly. Don't allow your house to fall into a state of disrepair.

Chapter 97

A Feature Film

I Ain't Over Until God Says It's Over."...

This is a true statement, BUT before WE decide that something is over, we need to find out if GOD has determined that it's over. There ARE times when "The End" of a situation a relationship actually IS the end, but then there are times when "The End" is not the finale, but an intermission leading into the next Act of a situation. Before we walk away from people or situations, we need to be sure that is what God desires.

God sees all aspects and angles of our situation. He has a view of the blind spots, the areas we don't see from the balcony, behind the camera, or from the orchestra pit. Before making a cut, before exiting the scene, before you decide to shut down the production of your film it's best to consult God, who is the director of your life! God very well may want a situation to end, but before you make moves to do so, take a moment to hear from God, to hear what HE wants from you! Perhaps His desire is not for you to take your final bow but to simply take a step back and wait for the new chapter, or the sequel to the film. In any event, don't move, don't make decisions, and don't burn bridges unless you are sure that God has specifically directed you to do. Take the time to receive God's script for your life, to study the stage directions, and see where on the stage He wants to place you or with whom He desires to be your co- star. You owe it to yourself not to shut down aspects of your film production without talking to The One who has the power to make your life a feature film!

Chapter 98

Swine's And Pearls Don't Mix

Matthew 7:6 (NIV) *"Do not give dogs what is sacred;*
do not throw your pearls to pigs. If you do, they may trample them
under their feet, and turn and tear you to pieces."

This morning as I was reflecting, The Lord dropped this statement into my spirit: "Protect your assignment; protect your gift." I repeated the statement in my head, and then God began to give me a word of wisdom, and what I take also as a warning. The things that God gives us or assigns to us are precious and require our protection. The gifts and assignments that God gives us should not be exposed to everyone!

I think back to when I had my son and how particular I was with who held him and who cared for him in my absence. Everyone did not have access to him, and even now almost 13 years later, I am still mindful of who has access to him. He is my gift and my assignment, and I will do what I have to do to keep him safe from potential hazards! Often, when God places a gift or mandate in our hands, instead of keeping it to ourselves, we expose it to people who on the surface may seem to care, but who in reality may not be on our team. They may appear to be excited or concerned for us, but inwardly they may harbor some things that work against us.

Thus, we expose our pearl, our gift, or our assignment to swine, to haters who behind the scenes, in the spirit realm are trampling over what God has placed in our care.

Some time ago I was given an assignment, an assignment that I KNEW was given to me but I didn't understand it fully. In seeking clarity, I made the error of talking to someone who I believed at the time would give me the understanding I needed. But as I was listening to them, I knew right away I had made a terrible mistake! Instead of seeking the guidance of THE ONE who had given the assignment, I had exposed my assignment, thus I made it difficult for me to execute it because some blocks were erected! Even now, as I still work hard at what God has told me to do, it is a struggle because access had been given to me for something I was to protect. It was something I have no choice but to take responsibility for, but something that I continue to press through to accomplish.

As I continued to listen to God ministering to me, He let me know that everything He gives, assigns, blesses us with isn't for everyone to participate in; some things are private been us and God, and to expose those things doesn't build up our spiritual reputation of trust with God! His ability to place things in our care comes into question! The lesson and the wisdom here is not to showcase everything God gives you, and to discern what is meant for the group and what is meant for your personal development! You must discern what should be shared later, and what is to hold on to indefinitely.

These are questions that only God can answer, and questions that only He should answer! How tragic is it to know that something was destroyed, that a pearl was crushed due to our lack of protecting it! It is natural to become excited when God places something in our care or assigns something to us, but self-control ought to direct us so we know what we are to do with what had been given. If God gives us a gift or assignment, it says God has placed His confidence in us. It now becomes our responsibility not to disappoint Him, or cause God to regret His decision to trust us!!

Chapter 99

Which One Are You?

Which one are you? Are you someone like Jesus who operated more out of grace and compassion? Or are you like a Pharisee who mainly operated out of criticism and judgment? Do you share wisdom and correction out of love, and do you seek to understand why people do what they do? Or doesn't it matter to you where people are and what they've experienced? Is your concern only to point out their shortcomings?

Do you build up or tear down? Do you encourage more or find fault more? Does spiritual meekness come through, or does an arrogant personality step forward? When we look in our spiritual mirror, who looks back at us? Who do you represent? Whose heart do you have? Whose agenda do you display? These questions are things to consider as we come in contact with and interact with God's people.

Chapter 100

Don't Give Up On God!

As I write this last piece, I want to end by encouraging you not to give up on God! Sometimes as we walk this journey we get tired, and we get frustrated. We ask God all sorts of questions: "When? Why? How?" "Who? What? Where?"

When we don't see things coming into alignment as we think it should, then fear, doubt, and distrust begins to surface. While we may not openly say it, the seeds of giving up are planted! For a moment, let me take you back to a place in your life when you were at your lowest. You were rebellious, insubordinate, you engaged in sin and did things your own way; you ignored God, turned your back, refused to listen, and disobeyed. But in your mess, in your soot, in your filth, God didn't give up on YOU!! We owe it to God to see us through impossible situations!

We owe it to God to allow Him to prove himself to us. We owe it to God to allow Him to show Himself as the mighty God that He is!! We owe it to God to let what He's declared to us to manifest. We need to let Him do what He said He was going to do. We owe God our trust. We owe God our belief. We owe God faith. WE OWE GOD!!!

Don't give up on a God who has NEVER given up on YOU!!!

Be Blessed!!
Andrea

In Loving Honor ....

On March 5, 2017, my dad Elder Ronald A. Jenkins released his last earthly breath and took in his first breath in the presence of The Lord.

For 7.5 years I had the honor of serving as my father's caregiver, it wasn't always easy and some nights I cried under the weight of it all, but to give my dad the gift of peace during his final years, I would do it all again!!

Unfortunately, neither of my parents were able to see the completion of this book but I know both of them are smiling with pride and I'm so excited that I am able to share within these pages many of the spiritual and life lessons they instilled in me.

I Love You Mom and Dad, continue resting in Christ ❤

Your Daughter Andrea

www.ingramcontent.com/pod-product-compliance
Lightning Source LLC
Chambersburg PA
CBHW021224090426
42740CB00006B/370